ALSO BY DAVE MCINTOSH

Terror in the Starboard Seat

The Seasons of My Youth

The Collectors

Ottawa Unbuttoned

When the Work's All Done This Fall

HIGH BLUE BATTLE

Edited and Annotated by

DAVE McINTOSH

Stoddart

First published in 1990 by
Stoddart Publishing Co. Limited
34 Lesmill Road
Toronto, Canada
M3B 2T6

CANADIAN CATALOGUING IN PUBLICATION DATA

McIntosh, Dave
    High blue battle: the war diary of no. 1 (401) Fighter
    Squadron, RCAF

ISBN 0-7737-2338-2

1. World War, 1939-1945 - Squadron histories- Canada
2. World War, 1939-1945 - Aerial operations, Canadian
3. World War, 1939-1945 - Personal narratives, Canadian
4. Canada. Royal Canadian Air Force. Fighter Squadron, no. 1 (401)
History. I. McIntosh, Dave

D792.C2H55   1990   940.54′4971   C89-090625-4

Typesetting: Tony Gordon Limited

Printed and bound in Canada on acid-free paper.

All photographs are from the Canadian Forces Photographic Unit.

For those who went,
and came not again

Glossary

a/a, or **ack-ack:** anti-aircraft fire
a/c: aircraft
A/C/M: air chief marshal
airscrew: propeller
ammo: ammunition
AOC: air officer commanding
ASR: air sea rescue
A/V/M: air vice marshal
bandit: enemy aircraft
batman: valet, usually shoe-shiner and button-polisher only
bounce: take unawares from higher altitude
bowser: gas refuelling truck
browned off: fed up
CB: confined to barracks
cinegun: camera synchronized to aircraft guns
circus: bomber support and cover
CO: commanding officer
deck: zero feet
DFC: Distinguished Flying Cross (for officers)
DFM: Distinguished Flying Medal (for non-commissioned officers; harder to win)
ditch: make forced landing on water
dispersal: one of widely separated areas around airfield where aircraft are parked; the crew hut at dispersal
do: any event, from combat to station dance; if unpleasant, shaky do
DO: dental officer
DO: Dornier (German aircraft)

dogfight: confused air battle

drink: the sea, usually the English Channel, the no-man's-land of WWII

DSO: Distinguished Service Order

duff: poor or bad

e/a: enemy aircraft

erk: aircraftsman

FA: fuck-all; *see also* SFA

flak: enemy anti-aircraft fire, from German *flugzeugabwehrkanone*

fix: position, or determination of position

F/L: flight lieutenant

flamer: vehicle destroyed in flames

F/O: flying officer

F/S: flight sergeant

funk-hole: slit trench

FW: Focke-Wulf (German aircraft)

gaggle: formation of aircraft

G/C: group captain

gen: information; pukka (good) or duff (bad)

glycol: engine coolant

go: an attempt

Goldfish Club: unofficial organization of survivors who have ditched or baled out in sea; badge is a winged fish

gong: medal

HE: Heinkel (German aircraft)

hit the silk: take to parachute; bale out

Jerry: German

joy: success

JU: Junkers (German aircraft)

kite: aircraft

LAC: leading aircraftsman

Luftwaffe: German air force

Mae West: life jacket with bulging front

mayday: distress signal, from French *m'aidez*

ME: Messerschmitt (German aircraft)

met: meteorological branch

m/g: machine-gun

MO: medical officer
MT: motor transport
nacelle: aircraft engine casing
NCO: non-commissioned officer
ops: operations
ORs: other ranks
OTU: operational training unit
pack up: quit
pancake: land
perspex: windscreen, purportedly shatterproof
petrol: gas
piece of cake: cinch
P/O: pilot officer
prang: crash
probable: enemy aircraft probably destroyed
PT: physical training
ramrod: short-range bomber raid
ranger: fighter sweep
recce: reconnaissance
rhubarb: low-level attack on ground targets
rodeo: fighter sweep
R/T: radio-telephone
scramble: quick take-off
SFA: sweet fuck-all; *see also* FA
Sgt: sergeant
S/L: squadron leader
smoker: vehicle enveloped in smoke but not seen in flames
snafu: a mess (situation normal, all fucked up)
sortie: operational flight by single aircraft
S/P: sergeant-pilot
u/s: unserviceable, whether people, machines or weather
V1: buzz bomb; German robot bomb
WAAF: Women's Auxiliary Air Force (RAF)
W/C: wing commander (also Wingco)
WD: Women's Division (RCAF)
WO: warrant officer (WO1, first class; WO2, second class)

RANKS OF THE RCAF, BOTTOM TO TOP

Other ranks (ORs)
AC2: aircraftsman, second class
AC1: aircraftsman, first class
LAC: leading aircraftsman
Cpl: Corporal
Sgt and S/P: sergeant and sergeant-pilot
F/S: flight sergeant
WO2: warrant officer, second class
WO1: warrant officer, first class

Officers
P/O: pilot officer
F/O: flying officer
F/L: flight lieutenant
S/L: squadron leader
W/C: wing commander
G/C: group captain
A/C: air commodore
A/V/M: air vice marshal
A/M: air marshal
A/C/M: air chief marshal

Airfield near London, early morning, during the Battle of Britain, 1940. Planes are Hurricanes of RCAF's No. 1 Fighter Squadron, the only Canadian unit (though not the only Canadians) in the battle. Aircraft were dispersed around the field to avoid presenting a mass target for German raiders.

Throughout the day, pilots waited near their planes for scramble (take-off) orders to go up to meet massive German attacks. They flew three or four combat sorties a day. They kept their Mae Wests (life jackets) on while pitching horseshoes, one of the few recreations at the dispersal point.

INTRODUCTION

WHEN HE WAS KILLED, aged nineteen, on December 11, 1941, while flying with 412 Squadron, Royal Canadian Air Force, in England, Pilot Officer John Gillespie Magee left us a poem, "High Flight," which is still widely quoted:

> Oh! I have slipped the surly bonds of earth
> And danced the skies on laughter-silvered wings.

He also left an unfinished poem he called "Per Ardua." He had time for only a first draft. The second verse goes

> Some that have left other mouths to tell the story
> Of high blue battle — quite young limbs that bled,
> How they had thundered up the clouds to glory
> Or fallen to an English field, stained red.

What better "other mouths to tell the story of high blue battle" than the airmen-diarists of the only Canadian fighter squadron to take part in the 1940 Battle of Britain and which saw continuous action after that until the conquest of Germany in 1945.

A daily diary was part of the official paperwork required of a squadron. Most wartime diaries are a mere recitation of numbers of aircraft, take-off and landing times, combat results and casualties. I gave up reading them after wading through the dry account of my own squadron, 418, until Glenn Wright of the National Archives drew my attention to the extraordinary qualities of the diary of No. 1 Fighter Squadron, RCAF. It differs from other logbooks in that it regularly comments, sometimes humorously, sometimes sarcastically, on many aspects of squadron life other than flying. There are lots of wine, women and song or, as one commanding officer noted on a remote, winter-bound station, wine, sleep and song.

Allow me to provide here an example of the diary's social commentary. In October 1940, No. 1 was pulled out of frontline action for a comparative rest at Prestwick, Scotland, where a number of Indians were also stationed. The squadron diarist noted that the Indians "constitute quite a problem as far as messing [feeding] is concerned. Different religions compel varied diets. There are also the troubles with pay and allowances, as some boast of six wives. These are looked on with envy by some of the more virile pilots and with awe by the older ones."

It seemed appropriate to me for several reasons that the diary of No. 1 should be published. For one thing, 1990 is the fiftieth anniversary of the Battle of Britain, and No. 1 was the only Canadian unit in it (but by no means the only Canadians). No. 1 was the highest-scoring fighter squadron in the RCAF, first with the Hawker Hurricane, then with the Vickers-Supermarine Spitfire.

For us today, the diary is a vivid re-creation of those wartime days — from the inside. And, as far as I know, this is the first time a Canadian squadron diary has been so published.

No. 1 was proud of being Canadian, though mercifully it never referred to itself as the "Fighting First." A frequent notation at the end of its monthly summary of activities was: "Percentage personnel RCAF: air crew, 100%; ground crew, 100%."

The juxtaposition of some entries in the diary may seem startling, even jarring, today. But that's the way the war was; there was no time for grieving. The station dance was not postponed or cancelled because a pilot, no matter how senior or well regarded, was killed or went missing. The pub crawl and the funeral were the two sides of the same coin.

The diarists are anonymous for the most part. Once in a while, the chronicler mentions that he is being or has been relieved by so-and-so during leave. The writers, it is clear from the text, were usually fliers, though in the later years the intelligence officer or adjutant might well have taken a hand. Often the diarist records an operation from which he has just returned. A casualty list or a posting claimed them all eventually. On November 13, 1940, the diarist says that F/O Bill Sprenger has been the writer for the last seven days and "Leave coming to an end, your regular scribe takes up the torch again." Thirteen days later, he records the death of Sprenger in a crash on the west bank of Loch Lomond.

The raw material for the diary was the debriefing of pilots after each operation — the word "mission" was seldom if ever used in the RCAF — and the pilots' combat reports. Debriefing was usually done by the Squadron intelligence officer. The pilot related where he'd been and what he'd done and the intelligence officer took notes. If an enemy plane had been shot down or damaged, a combat report had to be filled out and signed by the pilot. The reports generally are not prime examples of the literature of action and adventure; they are understated and conform to a rigid format: location, height, length of machine-gun and cannon burst, distance and angle, observed strikes and so on. Any words which could not be found in a grade school primer were officially frowned on.

For two years, No. 1 Squadron (renumbered 401 in 1941) kept two diaries. An unofficial one was typed on foolscap; the other was the official record of operations on the prescribed official, oblong form. The official logbook recorded all flights and technical details and took in as much of the unofficial diary as the author deemed fit. The latter diary, which was preserved along with the authorized version, was kept between September 7, 1940, and September 6, 1942. Parts of the unofficial diary were apparently dropped in the official one, for reasons of space and not laziness. On many days, when there was little of note, the diary entries must have been a considerable chore.

The diary covers every single day, but I have dropped numerous entries which are, perforce, repetitive, routine and dull. Entries from both diaries, official and unofficial, have been combined. None of the words of the diarists has been changed, though spellings, capitalization and abbreviations have been made consistent. Explanations have been inserted where considered necessary, as well as some incidental, relevant material.

The entries are those their young Canadian authors wrote half a century ago in the frenzy and boredom of war. The Squadron flew every single day, weather permitting — and the weather had to be awful to prevent flying — on operations, routine patrols and training. The gaps in the diary dates here do not signify idleness; they say only that there wasn't much doing out of the ordinary on those days, militarily or socially.

The glossary is confined to words and expressions used in the diary. Many expressions were borrowed from the Royal Air Force, which seems only fair because the RAF borrowed liberally from Canadians, one of the best known examples being "fucked by the fickle finger of fate." (The complete expression is "fucked by the five fickle fingers of fate, dashed by the deadly digits of destiny, screwed, blued and tattooed, all in one go.") British etymologist Eric Partridge also ascribes to Canadian sources such delicate terms as "poontang," for copulation; "poor man's piano," for a meal of beans; "have one's tit in a tight crack"; "fart in a windstorm"; "fuck like a mink"; and "fucking the dog." The diary contains none of these, but it does have FA and SFA (see glossary). One day during the Battle of Britain a German raider got through to No. 1's airfield without warning and bombed two hangars, killing two airmen. The diarist attributes the failure to defend the field to a "God damn bloody awful balls-up" — and immediately adds "apologies to the padre and any others who object."

No. 1 was formed March 1, 1937, at Trenton, Ontario. The first entry in its diary was made June 15 that year: "Routine flight duties." The early entries were always bareboned. The Squadron's first aircraft were Armstrong-Whitworth Siskin biplanes. In February 1939, seven single-wing Hurricane fighters were shipped in crates from England to Vancouver, re-assembled there and flown by Squadron pilots to Calgary, where the Squadron was then based.

At the outbreak of the war in September 1939, No. 1 moved to St. Hubert, near Montreal. They were given three more Hurricanes, grabbing one from the Canadian National Exhibition in Toronto where it was on static display. Two months later the

Squadron flew (in three laps) to Dartmouth, Nova Scotia, across the harbor from Halifax. There it was amalgamated in May 1940 with 115 Fighter Squadron of Montreal, an auxiliary unit of weekend and two-weeks-in-summer fliers. No. 115 had formed in 1936 but had never flown Hurricanes. No. 1 was further augmented by members of 8, 10 and 11 Bomber Reconnaissance squadrons, all based in Nova Scotia. The regular RCAF squadrons represented a cross-section of Canadians, but 115 comprised Montrealers almost exclusively, and they predominated in the Squadron's fight in the Battle of Britain.

In June 1940, the Squadron crated its Hurricanes and sailed in a convoy to England. The Canadian Army's 1st Canadian Division was already in Britain and the intention was that No. 1 Squadron, along with No. 110 Army Co-operation Squadron, in Britain since February 1940, would provide its air support. But the German blitzkrieg through the Netherlands, Belgium and France preempted any 1st Division move to the continent, and No. 1 was pitched into the Battle of Britain in August.

Squadron Leader E.A. (Ernie) McNab of Regina, the commanding officer, was a stubby and stubborn man and he insisted that his inexperienced pilots be allowed a decent interval for operational training. This was gained mostly at Croydon near London, already well known to international air travellers. To help gain experience himself, McNab flew with 111 Squadron of the RAF and on August 11, 1940, shot down a Dornier 17 bomber over Westgate-on-Sea. It was not the first air victory of the war by an RCAF pilot, however. That occurred May 25, 1940, and belonged to S/L F.M. Gobeil when he commanded the RAF's 242 Squadron. (No. 242 continued as an all-Canadian squadron except for its commanding officer when Douglas Bader, the legless British ace, took it over.) Many Canadians had joined the RAF before the war and in early 1940 there were some 2,400 of them, air and ground crew, in RAF units. The first victory by a Canadian was by F/O Howard Peter Blatchford, who shared the destruction of a Heinkel-111 on October 17, 1939.

No. 1's main base of operations in the Battle of Britain was Northolt aerodrome just northwest of London. Its personnel comprised 27 officers, 21 of them pilots, and 314 airmen to fly and maintain twenty Hurricanes, including spares, which were quickly used up. An airborne squadron consisted of twelve planes in four sections, divided, for maintenance purposes, into A and B flights.

After a disastrous beginning in the battle, when it shot down two RAF coastal patrol planes, the Squadron scored its first success August 26 by downing three Dorniers and damaging three more. McNab shot down one and had to crash-land. F/L Gordon McGregor, later to become president of Trans-Canada Air Lines (Air Canada), got another. F/O R.L. Edwards, McNab's No. 2 in Blue Section, shot the tail off a German bomber, but its gunners hit him and he spun down out of control and was killed. F/O Hartland de M. Molson, later a senator, and F/O A.D. Nesbitt each damaged one German plane. F/O J.P.J. Desloges, like McNab, made a forced landing.

In mid-August, the Luftwaffe had begun an all-out assault on the airfields of southeast England in an attempt to knock the RAF out of the war. It was not unusual for No. 1 on return from combat to find that its field, whether Northolt or an alternative, had been bombed. The ground crew was sometimes in almost as much danger as the pilots while they worked through the disruption and debris to repair, refuel and re-arm the Hurricanes. The Squadron was often assigned to strictly aerodrome defence while it could clearly see huge daylight attacks on London. McNab once became so frustrated with this order that he streaked off independently and shot down a German raider.

The Squadron put up three and sometimes four patrols a day, usually morning, noon and afternoon, and sometimes evening, and with night raids on the airfield besides, nobody got much sleep. "The night was made hideous with loud bangs," the Squadron diarist noted September 28.

Many of the pilots had to bale out at least once but, if not wounded, went right back up again the next day. They were like cheeky kids playing king of the castle. They would have been back up the same day but their parachute landings were always too far from base to allow quick return to the Squadron. Most of the wounds were severe burns to face, hands and legs caused by quick-starting fires set by enemy machine-guns and cannon. At one period, No. 1 had six pilots in hospital at the same time. Casualties were called "non-effectives" and sometimes appeared in the monthly summary under the heading of "postings," whether to the hospital or to the grave.

Reinforcements were scarce, if available at all, and once (September 27) the Squadron could muster only six planes, half its usual strength, for the day's third patrol. The six shot down five bombers. By the end of the day, says the diary, "The Squadron was a very tired, unshaven group of warriors." Ten days later, the Squadron medical officer reported "strain and general tiredness."

Despite such strain, the diarist took time to lampoon the British Commonwealth Air Training Plan, officially signed December 17, 1939, to produce 25,000 aircrew a year, mostly Canadians and mainly for the RAF. The plan also called for construction of sixty new airfields in Canada, additions to the existing twenty, and seventy training schools, depots and other buildings. The diary noted that the plan wouldn't produce any pilots until January 1941, which, it added, doubtless satisfied the Germans.

By 1944, nearly thirty per cent of RAF aircrew were Canadians. (The percentage had been nearly fifty in the Royal Flying Corps in the First World War.) This huge Canadian component in the RAF was in addition to the forty Canadian squadrons in Britain. Canadians who served in the RAF have since been officially ignored by the British government because they were Canadians, and officially by the Canadian government because they were in British, not Canadian, squadrons. Only one person, as far as I know, has tried to rectify this historical oversight. With his own money and after years of research, Les Allison of Roland, Manitoba, published in 1978 a book entitled *Canadians in the Royal Air Force*. One page stands by itself in Canadian publishing. Headed "Non Acknowledgements," it castigates the Canada Council, Canadian and British defence departments and twenty Royal Canadian Legion branches for refusing to help Allison in his research.

During the Battle of Britain, the No. 1 pilots spent nearly all their daylight hours — they didn't take up night-fighting until much later, and then only briefly — at dispersal points around the airfield where their planes were parked ready for a quick getaway. The wooden dispersal hut was primitive, almost squalid, and contained a few sticks of furniture and a telephone to receive flight orders. The telephone was used until the Tannoy (public address) system was introduced later. The pilots "lay around with telephones ringing in their bellies," in a phrase of the time, as they waited for the shrill summons to high blue battle. On sunny days they sat outside on rickety chairs or on the ground, some reading, some playing cards, some pitching horse-shoes.

Aloft, the Squadron wasn't deterred by odds. It was often out-numbered four to one when it tore into German formations of bombers and their fighter screens. F/O O.J. Peterson of Lloydminster, Saskatchewan, on September 9 attacked an ME-109 fighter so fiercely and at such close range that fragments of glass and perspex cut his face open and the blood obscured his vision. He couldn't see his instruments and fell to 1,500 feet before he was able to recover. Peterson was killed September 27 when the Squadron attacked thirty German bombers escorted by some twenty-five ME-109 and ME-110 fighters.

Throughout the Battle of Britain, which didn't end until well into 1941 when the Germans gave up their plans for a sea invasion of England, No. 1 Squadron flew the Hurricane fighter. The plane could not gain much altitude and its maximum speed was only 335 miles an hour. It was armed with the Browning machine-gun, four in each wing. Although the Spitfire was faster (the Mark I had a maximum speed of 367 miles an hour) and a better climber, the Squadron wasn't re-equipped with it until the fall of 1941. The early Spitfire carried the same armament as the Hurricane. Later models were armed with 20-millimetre cannon as well as machine-guns and were much faster. Both the Hurricane and the Spitfire were powered by the Rolls-Royce Merlin engine. With its elliptical wing, the Spitfire was often called the most beautiful fighter ever built (if one can think of warplanes as possessing beauty).

In the fifty-three days it was in the battle, No. 1 shot down thirty German planes, probably destroyed eight and damaged thirty-five. It lost three pilots killed (F/Os Edwards, R. Smither and Peterson), ten wounded and sixteen Hurricanes. It won three Distinguished Flying Crosses (S/L McNab, F/L McGregor and F/O Russel), the first gallantry awards to members of the RCAF in the Second World War. The most successful day — and it remained so until the air battle over the Normandy beaches in June and July 1944 — was September 27, 1940, when the Squadron destroyed seven planes (reduced from eleven by shared kills with pilots of other squadrons), probably destroyed another and damaged three. Thirteen pilots flew twenty-six sorties and engaged seventy enemy aircraft that day. Six of them flew three sorties each within seven hours.

Nearly all the No. 1 pilots shot done at least one enemy in the Battle of Britain. McGregor destroyed five; Russel destroyed four and shared another. McGregor, Russel, Nesbitt and other No. 1 pilots went on to help form, lead and command other Canadian fighter squadrons, wings and groups before the war ended. Russel flew three tours of operations, one of the few fighter pilots in the RCAF to do so.

Red tape was a constant irritant. At the height of the Battle of Britain, RCAF headquarters issued orders to No. 1 that sweaters and scarves were not to be worn in place of collars and ties. The diarist suggested that each pilot would have to be sartorially inspected as he leaped into his plane to go up to meet the King's enemies. Later, there were regulations which forbade tucking trousers into flying boots. A 1941 diarist noted that headquarters in London could always be relied upon for volunteers for a squadron dance, but never for a funeral. At one station, the most senior RCAF officer overseas inspected the typewriters in the orderly room and decreed one surplus. Spare parts for a type of plane the Squadron didn't fly would arrive. A draft of ground crew would show up unannounced. There was a constant stream of niggling questions from headquarters: it says here on Form 541 that twelve planes took off but the names of only eleven pilots are listed. Personal mail was censored. Headquarters snitched on one airman because he had told his family in a letter home that he had scrounged a pailful of coal; on another because he had won £4 gambling, officially not permitted but which went on constantly, as the diary shows.

Living conditions varied widely from base to base. At some RAF stations, there were adequate quarters for both pilots and ground crew. But at most there were cold and damp Nissen huts, abandoned camps and even barns. The Squadron lived a great deal of the time under canvas, especially after the Normandy invasion in June 1944, when it moved to France. It acclimatized beforehand by living in tents in southern England. No matter the cover, nearly all the maintenance work on the aircraft was done outdoors in all weather and in all seasons.

The two worst stretches were the winter of 1940-41 at Castletown in the northeast corner of Scotland, where the first baths could not be arranged for three weeks, and the fall of 1944 in Holland when, the diarist said, the little Dutch boy must have taken his finger out of the hole in the dyke. At Castletown the Squadron was supposed to be helping guard the fleet at Scapa Flow in the Orkneys, but spent most of its time shovelling snow and keeping the eight-mile road open between billets and airfield.

In all, the Squadron moved thirty-three times; the men sometimes felt like a group of tourists, in the words of the diary. The Squadron became so adept at the transfers that it could change bases in a day while remaining fully operational.

During lulls in combat — war is hurry up and wait — there was time in 1941, 1942 and 1943, while the Allies gathered their strength for the assault on Europe, for the Squadron chroniclers to take note of the pilots' off-duty escapades with women and drink. There was, for instance, the "certain amount of unpleasantness with the [pub] management over the breaking of their glasses." Roughhouses were fairly common in No. 1's mess. Their usual feature was a human pyramid so that footprints could be implanted on the ceiling. There are frequent and ribald references to women, such as "Three-Guinea Gwen" in Lincoln, a naked blonde loose in the pilots' quarters but too plastered to be of any use to anybody and an entertainer "who dangled everything." The diarist belabors an airman who forgot his rubbers (condoms) and tried to borrow one at the crucial moment.

The difference in rank between officers and non-commissioned officers (the so-called "other ranks") could be a problem from time to time but never seems to have been a serious one on No. 1 Squadron. Any pilot who pulled rank on his ground crew, on or off station, was asking for trouble; not that spanners were deliberately left in the works, but the plane of a heartily disliked pilot might well not receive the detailed attention and loving care of that of a popular officer. There are numerous references in the No. 1 diary to beer parties by air and ground crew together, especially in the dispersal hut at the end of the day. Traditionally, the officers waited on table for the men at Christmas dinner. But the British pub served as the great common social ground for Canadian officers and men. Squadrons always shared airfields with two or three other squadrons, and many RCAF disciplinary problems arose because of RAF station commanders who were sticklers for authority.

The most difficult problem of all was the formal division in rank among the pilots themselves: some were officers, some were not. Officers lived in different (and better) quarters than non-commissioned officers, that is, the sergeant-pilots they flew with day after day. Though there were rare exceptions, sergeants could not join the officers in the latter's mess in the evening to chew the battle fat; by the same token, officers were barred from the sergeants' mess except in special circumstances. Generally, the Air Force's solution was to promote sergeant-pilots to officer rank at the first opportunity, such as outstanding airmanship in combat. The drawback was that it made it more difficult to win the Distinguished Flying Medal. The DFM was awarded to non-commissioned officers, the Distinguished Flying Cross to officers. In many instances, a deserving non-commissioned airman was given promotion to officer rank instead of the DFM. Besides, it was much simpler for a squadron commander to recommend promotion than write out a citation for a medal. Only 515 DFMs were awarded to RCAF members during the Second World War compared with 4,017 DFCs.

In March 1941, the Squadron was redesignated 401, when the RAF allotted the numbers 400 to 448 to Canadian squadrons to avoid confusion with RAF units. Two months later, the Squadron received what were supposed to be new Hurricanes and found insecure patches over bullet holes. In September 1941, the Squadron converted to the Spitfire V-B and kept that type of plane till the end of the war. While 401 was getting Spitfires, the Luftwaffe brought into service the FW-190 fighter.

The Squadron began fighter sweeps over France, challenging the Germans to come up (mostly, they didn't), and escort duties for Allied bombers on daylight raids. Later, it turned to rhubarbs, low-level attacks on ground targets. And all the while, it was still responsible for its original role, the air defence of Britain.

The Squadron's worst day occurred only a month after it was re-equipped with Spitfires. While flying with two RAF Squadrons, it was "bounced" over France by some fifty FW-190s and ME-109s and lost three pilots killed and two others shot down and taken prisoner.

What the Squadron later termed its riskiest operation — the entire squadron was nearly lost — was flown September 26, 1942. It was escorting bombers to Britanny at 24,000 feet. The wind from the north was much stronger than predicted — 100 mph against a forecast 34 mph — and the Squadron nearly didn't make it back to England; it lost one pilot who ran out of fuel over the English Channel. One RAF squadron accompanying 401 became so deranged by the unexpected wind strength that part of it tried to land in Britanny, mistaking it for southwest England; the entire squadron (No. 133) was lost except for one pilot who crash-landed on the English coast.

The previous month, 133 had flown with 401 as cover for American Fortress bombers supporting the 2nd Canadian Division raid on Dieppe. Once the escort job was done, 401 turned on the German bombers and fighters attacking the Canadian troops and their convoy ships. There were dogfights throughout a good part of the day. F/O Don Morrison of Toronto shot down an FW-190 before being forced to bale out over the Channel. He was picked up by a rescue launch and spent the rest of the day helping to rescue others, both downed pilots and survivors of other launches set afire by German planes.

The Squadron spent January to May 1943 in Yorkshire before returning to 11 Group command in southeast England, where most of the action was. It continued its mayhem in the air and against ground targets (mostly trains) as preparations were made for the Allied assault on Fortress Europe. In some ways, it was like Battle of Britain days. F/L Ian Ormston baled out over the Channel one morning and was back in time for lunch. F/O K.B. Woodhouse baled out over France southeast of Amiens and was back in ten days, having evaded capture. F/O R.M. (Tex) Davenport baled out over France in January and returned in April; in August he crash-landed in France and returned in a day.

On D-Day, June 6, 1944, the pilots were wakened at 3:15 a.m. in their tents at Tangmere on the south coast of England. They beat up enemy transport that day, but their main job was protecting the Normandy beaches, including the Canadian landing beach Juno, against German air attack. The next day the Squadron destroyed seven JU-88s trying to bomb the beachhead and one FW-190 fighter. It was its highest one-day toll in planes destroyed since the Battle of Britain four years earlier. F/S R.D. Davidson, who had joined 401 only two days earlier, went missing. In listing his name, the monthly summary added "of whom nothing is known." That was the fate — to this day — of many Squadron pilots.

On June 18, the Squadron moved to B-4 airfield at Beny-sur-mer, France, dug slit trenches and put up tents and a portable hangar. It was the ground crew's job to stand guard around the airfield, time permitting, and frightened cows were often challenged by nervous sentries. The field was close to the front line of the land battle.

On July 20, the Squadron scored its 100th victory. A week later, in two dogfights, it destroyed nine enemy aircraft — seven ME-109s and two FW-190s.

The Squadron lost one commanding officer after another, but sometimes not for long. S/L Lorne Cameron was brought down by flak behind enemy lines July 3 and was replaced by Middle East veteran S/L I.F. (Hap) Kennedy. Kennedy was hit by flak and baled out July 26; he evaded capture and walked into camp August 24. In the meantime, S/L H.C. Trainor had replaced Kennedy and on July 27 shot down one of nine German planes destroyed by the Squadron that day. Trainor was knocked down by flak August 18 and returned a week later; he baled out again September 19 and was taken prisoner. F/L Scotty Murray was shot down June 28, returned August 14 after evading capture and reported that while in hiding he'd run into S/L Cameron in a hayloft. F/L A.F. Halcrow went the evaders one better after he baled out and was captured; he persuaded his German captors to let him go on the understanding that he would arrange for their quiet surrender to Allied troops.

The long years of operations — and continual training — made 401 vastly superior to the Luftwaffe pilots and planes in the last months of the war. For the second time, on September 29, 1944, the Squadron destroyed nine enemy planes in a single day. The ferocity of the air war is shown in a combat report by F/L J.H. Everard (later shot down and captured while commanding officer): "I gave this [ME-109] two 2-second bursts from seventy-five yards quarter astern. On the second burst it exploded and I was unable to steer clear of the debris. Part of the pilot's body hit my mainplane inboard of the starboard cannon and dented it. Superficial damage."

The 401 pilots could out-duel even the new German jet fighter, the ME-262. Led by S/L R.I.A. Smith of Regina, the commanding officer, they shot down the first ME-262 destroyed by the Allies on October 31, 1944. Smith reported: "He flew at very high speed and I managed to get behind him and fire two 3-second bursts at 200/300 yards. He zoomed very high and I saw strikes on him in the port and starboard nacelles. A small fire started in the starboard nacelle and then a big one in the port nacelle while I was firing. He crashed in a field about two miles southwest of Nijmegen."

The Squadron always wanted to be as close as possible to the front line to afford maximum support and protection for the army, and it had to move fast and often to keep up with the advancing Allied ground forces in the rush across France and the Low Countries to the Rhine. In these moves, the ground crew had the best of it, for a change. They had to go by road, affording them the opportunity to accept the cheers and small gifts of the liberated French, Belgians and Dutch. The Squadron loved Brussels. The diarist mentioned its amenities in this order: hot baths, ice cream, wine, women and song.

On Christmas day, 1944, the Squadron shot down two German planes and on New Year's Day, 1945, nine more, the third time it had destroyed nine in one day. On April 20, 1945, Hitler's birthday, the Squadron ran up the phenomenal score of eighteen enemy aircraft destroyed and six damaged. The commanding officer, S/L W.T. Klersy, destroyed three and shared in destruction of another. Klersy led the Squadron with 14½ German planes destroyed. Two weeks after the war ended, he was killed in an unexplained flying accident.

In the Northwest Europe campaign — that is, from D-Day on — 401 was one of three squadrons in 126 Canadian Wing, which, in turn, was one of three fighter wings in 83 Canadian Group of 2nd Tactical Air Force. It led the Group in sorties flown and planes destroyed.

During the war, No. 1/401 flew 10,527 operational sorties, destroyed 195½ enemy planes, probably destroyed 35 and damaged 140, the highest score of any Canadian fighter squadron. Nineteen of its pilots won the Distinguished Flying Cross, five a Bar to the DFC, and one (Don Morrison) the Distinguished Flying Medal. The Squadron battle honors are Battle of Britain, Defence of Britain, English Channe-North Sea, Dieppe, Fortress Europe, Normandy, Arnhem, France and Germany. Its badge is a Rocky Mountain sheep — near the end of the war the Squadron referred to itself as the Rams — and its motto, *mors celerrima hostibus,* or "terribly swift death to the enemy."

Fifty-three Squadron pilots were killed and eighteen taken prisoner. One of those killed was Sgt H.M. Batters of Portage la Prairie, Manitoba. Two days after Christmas 1942, the Squadron received a letter from Barbara Gardiner. She wrote, "Hank and I were to have been married . . . and it seems as if the whole world has crashed."

The Squadron was operating in Germany when the war ended. The entry in the diary for June 23 says, "A signal was received stating 401 was disbanded as of this date."

I am indebted to Glenn Wright of the National Archives of Canada, Ottawa, for leading me to the diary of No. 1 Fighter Squadron and pointing out its superior qualities.

I also wish to acknowledge permission of Norman Hillmer, acting director of the Directorate of History, National Defence Headquarters, to use the diary and ancillary material; and of Laddie Lucas to quote from his book *Wings of War* part of the Magee poem "Per Ardua." All the photos were supplied by the Canadian Forces Photographic Unit and printed by the Photo Centre of the Department of Supply and Services.

I also wish to thank the versatile Michael Martchenko of Toronto, illustrator of children's books, for the cover painting; and Gilles Desormeaux of the manuscript division of the National Archives (again) for his untiring help.

1939 - 1940

CALGARY, ALBERTA

August 25, 1939 All leave and passes cancelled.

August 30 Loading boxcars.

August 31 Squadron proceeds east.

September 3 (Sunday) War declared by the United Kingdom on Germany.

ST. HUBERT, QUEBEC

September 10 Orders received from National Defence Headquarters, Ottawa, instructing No. 1 (F) Squadron, St. Hubert, Quebec, to mobilize.

September 11 Squadron placed on war basis and mobilization was commenced.

September 16 F/L E.A. McNab proceeded to Toronto by rail for purpose of testing and ferrying Hurricane 329, which was on static display at Toronto Exhibition, to St. Hubert.

September 22 F/O E.M. Reyno flew Hurricane 316 at 16,000 feet for experience with oxygen equipment.

September 28 F/O E.L. Beach and thirty-seven airmen, balance of personnel at Calgary, reported to St. Hubert for duty, bringing strength of the Squadron up to five officers and seventy-two airmen.

November 1 Squadron handed over by S/L E.G. Fullerton to S/L E.A. McNab.

November 3 Seven Hurricanes departed for Dartmouth, Nova Scotia, via Rimouski, staying overnight at Moncton, New Brunswick.

DARTMOUTH, NOVA SCOTIA

November 20 Hurricane 329 crashed and pilot F/O D.R. Anderson was killed. F/O Reyno [did] diving attacks on naval vessels in Bedford Basin for anti-aircraft defence practice.

December 22 Escort to convoy.

February 2, 1940 One NCO supplied for week's duty on anti-sabotage guard at main gate.

April 14 Church parade Protestants. Confessions Roman Catholics. Three Hurricanes formation flying.

April 29 Annual revolver practice.

May 22 Advice received that Squadron to proceed overseas. Inoculations and vaccinations for officers completed.

May 23 Complete kit inspection of all ranks. Crating [of Hurricanes] continued.

May 31 Armbands "Canada" issued to personnel not already in possession of same.

June 8 Squadron paraded in full marching order at 1600 hours. Boarded steamship E37 [*Duchess of Atholl*] in Halifax at 1900 hours. Assigned quarters.

June 9 Machine-gun posts No. 1 and 2 on bridge assigned to Squadron for voyage.

June 11 Departed Halifax at 1000 hours under escort of three destroyers and one battleship. A patrol of Stranraer aircraft accompanied the convoy until dusk.

IN CONVOY

June 12 Physical training at 1000 hours. Payday for troops —
£1 per man.

LIVERPOOL, ENGLAND

June 20 Squadron arrived at Liverpool and disembarked at
1530 hours. Departed Liverpool at 1630 hours, spending the
night at RAF Station Wheaton.

It was reported by one officer that squadron members sang as
they rode the tender from the *Duchess of Atholl* to dockside. The
words given for two songs appear considerably cleaned up. As
officially written, they were:

Canada's fighter squadron
From the shores of Canada we have come
To put old Hitler on his bum
We'll take the thug, and flatten his mug,
We're Canada's fighter squadron.
CHORUS:
Away, away with plane and gun
Here we come, Number One,
Seeking the Hun to put on the run,
We're Canada's fighter squadron.

A fighter's dream
As I was sitting in my plane,
Warming the motors up a bit,
Suddenly the thought went thru my brain
That I'd like to down a Messerschmitt.
CHORUS:
Tiddly-I-O, Tiddly-I-A
Tiddly-I-O for Number One
Rub-a-dub-dub fighters all,
Hi jig-a-jig très bon.

MIDDLE WALLOP, ENGLAND

June 21 Arrived RAF Station Middle Wallop 2000 hours.

June 22 Some of the Squadron are billeted out and some personnel are living under canvas as the station is under construction.

June 25 The Squadron was visited by Air Chief Marshal Sir Hugh Dowding [of RAF's Fighter Command]. The pilots were introduced to him. He also inquired as to what degree of training the Squadron had reached. When the A/C/M was told that the Squadron's Hurricanes [then being uncrated and re-assembled] were not of the latest type, he immediately made arrangements to replace these aircraft with new Hurricanes. [This was done June 30.]

June 26 First practice flight in this country was carried out by F/L G.R. McGregor and F/O C.E. Briese in two Harvard aircraft.

June 27 The first air-raid alarm occurred during the night, a stick of bombs being dropped in the vicinity of the station.

July 4 Squadron departed Middle Wallop and arrived at RAF Station Croydon at 1900 hours.

CROYDON, ENGLAND

July 16 Aircraft being prepared with proper markings, YO being the Squadron prefix with A-Z indicating individual a/c.

August 2 Bomber interceptions were practised.

August 8 Anti-gas lectures were delivered to members of the Squadron.

August 11 S/L McNab while attached on an operational flight with No. 111 Squadron shot down a Dornier 17.

August 16 Squadron preparing to move to Northolt from Croydon.

NORTHOLT, ENGLAND

August 24 Squadron were sent on an interception but returned to base, having landed at Tangmere to refuel.

The operations record book did not tell the true and terrible events of August 24, 1940, the only occasion when unpalatable facts were overlooked. The Squadron shot down two Blenheim patrol planes of 235 Squadron RAF Coastal Command, mistaking them for German JU-88 bombers. McNab and F/O P.B. Pitcher recognized the planes as friendly when the interception was made off Portsmouth, but others did not. F/L McGregor and F/O J.P.J. Desloges together claimed a JU-88 destroyed and F/Os A.D. Nesbitt, Arthur Yuile and W.P. Sprenger claimed hits on another JU-88. The pilots said they had been fired on, but the Blenheims had been shooting yellow and red Very pistol flares to identify themselves as friendly. One Blenheim crashed into the sea and the three-man crew was killed. The other crashlanded and the crew got out with cuts and bruises. It was a tragic introduction for No. 1 Squadron into the Battle of Britain. RCAF Headquarters in London did not tell National Defence in Ottawa about it until after the war, on February 27, 1947, and then only in reply to an official query. The letter from London said,

> The five combat reports submitted by No. 1 Canadian Squadron, dated 24 August, 1940, and queried in your referenced letter, were unsubstantiated claims. The two aircraft destroyed in these combats were Blenheims of Coastal Command.
> Documents giving the full story of the mistaken attacks are enclosed.
> Two versions of the Operations Record Book of No. 1 Canadian Squadron for the month of August, 1940,

are in existence. One version described the attack on the Coastal Command aircraft on August 24, but implies that it was broken off before any damage was done. This version of the Operations Record Book omits any mention of the genuine Squadron victories on August 26 and August 31. The second version of the Operations Record Book omits all mention of the attack on August 24, but describes the action on August 26 [and 31].

It is the second version which survives in the files of the defence department's history directorate and in the microfilm copy in the National Archives.

August 26 Shortly before 1500 hours the Squadron was again ordered on patrol and after several vectors a formation of twenty-five to thirty DO-215s was sighted at about 15,000 feet. A formation of escorting German fighters was drawn off by a Spitfire squadron. In the ensuing battle our Squadron accounted for six Dorniers, three destroyed and three severely damaged. These were credited to the Squadron as a whole. Heavy crossfire was experienced and three of our aircraft were shot down, two of which force-landed safely with S/L McNab and F/O Desloges, but the third crashed with F/O R.L. Edwards and he was killed.

August 31 While patrolling the coast [near Dover] a number of ME-109s attacked out of the sun. Only two of our fighters managed to bring their sights on the enemy for quick bursts but no claims were made. F/L V.B. Corbett and F/Os George Hyde and Sprenger all baled out safely. F/L Corbett and F/O Hyde were burned about the face, hands and legs but F/O Sprenger escaped injury. At 1730 hours another scramble took place and the Squadron intercepted fifty bombers escorted by a large formation of fighters. The battle took place near Gravesend and our attack was hampered by a/a fire but met with a certain amount of success. Two ME-109s were destroyed by F/Os B.E. (Bev) Christmas and

Flying Officer Hartland de M. Molson of No. 1 Fighter Squadron catches a moment's rest in the dispersal hut while waiting for the telephone call to action. He was appointed to the Senate in 1955.

Pilots of No. 1 Fighter Squadron race to their planes on orders to scramble. In early October 1940, the squadron medical officer reported that the pilots were suffering from "strain and general tiredness."

Hurricane "D" (the letters YO were the Squadron's identification) of No. 1 Squadron taxis from dispersal at Northolt airfield, northwest of London. Northolt was the Squadron's main base during the Battle of Britain.

Hurricanes roll along the perimeter track toward the runway.

An example of No. 1 Squadron's most formidable antagonist, the Messerschmitt 109, has been brought down in a grainfield in southern England. No. 1 shot down thirty German planes during the Battle of Britain for the loss of three pilots killed and ten wounded.

A Hurricane being refuelled from a bowser. Ground crew repaired, re-armed and refuelled the fighters as fast as possible in preparation for the next scramble. Machine-guns were often still hot from firing when the fighters returned to base to reload and refuel.

Nearly all maintenance work on fighter squadrons was done outdoors in all seasons. A tot of rum was sometimes the reward for ground crew after a dawn-to-dusk day in rain or snow.

Squadron Leader E.A. (Ernie) McNab of Regina, the commanding officer of No. 1 Fighter Squadron during the Battle of Britain.

The official photo of S/L E.A. McNab wearing the Distinguished Flying Cross, the first awarded to a member of the RCAF in the Second World War. Many other Canadians flew with the Royal Air Force during the Battle of Britain and one RAF squadron, No. 242, was all Canadian.

A group of No. 1 officers around S/L E.A. McNab. From left: F/O W.P. Sprenger, F/O O.J. Peterson, F/L W.R. Pollock, F/O P.B. Pitcher, McNab, F/O P.W. Lochnan, F/L E.M. Reyno, F/O E.W. Beardmore, F/O S.T. Blaiklock and F/O R.W. Norris. Peterson was killed in the Battle of Britain.

Flying Officer D.B. (Dal) Russel, DFC, of Montreal, one of Canada's top fighter pilots during the Second World War. He began by destroying German planes while flying with No. 1 in the Battle of Britain, and went on to command other squadrons and wings.

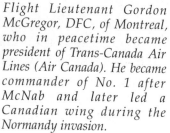

Flight Lieutenant Gordon McGregor, DFC, of Montreal, who in peacetime became president of Trans-Canada Air Lines (Air Canada). He became commander of No. 1 after McNab and later led a Canadian wing during the Normandy invasion.

T.B. Little and one damaged by F/O R. Smither while one DO-215 was destroyed by F/O J.W. Kerwin and one damaged by F/O D.B. (Dal) Russel. F/O Desloges baled out with quite severe burns about the face, hands and legs.

September 1 A raid consisting of about twenty to thirty bombers with a large fighter screen was intercepted at 1415 hours over Biggin Hill at 18,000 feet. The Squadron attacked and one DO-215 was destroyed and one damaged by F/L McGregor and three others damaged by F/Os O.J. Peterson, Christmas and Kerwin. F/O Kerwin also damaged an ME-110 but was in turn shot down and baled out with face and hand burns.

September 2 F/L Corbett and F/Os Desloges, Kerwin and Hyde posted as non-effectives.

September 4 A visit was paid to the Squadron by Canadian press men and while they were looking at dispersal a scramble occurred at 1300 hours. The Squadron was vectored onto a formation of about twelve or fifteen ME-110s or Jaguars at 15,000 feet near East Grinstead. The enemy formed a protective circle but our height advantage enabled us to position ourselves before attacking with the result that two e/a were destroyed by F/Os Smither and Nesbitt, one probably destroyed by F/O Russel and five others damaged, two by F/O H. de M. Molson, and one each by F/L McGregor and F/Os Peterson and Smither. F/O Russel also damaged a JU-88. We suffered no casualties.

September 5 The Squadron was scrambled three times during the day without incident. High enemy fighter formations were in their usual position but kept their distance and we were unable to attack as our a/c were unable to reach their ceiling. [The Hurricane was very sluggish at 20,000 feet and above.]

September 7   There were a large number of e/a converging on London, estimated at over 400. The Squadron did not have the opportunity of engaging enemy as our duty was aerodrome defence. Heavy a/a fire was observed over London and fires started by incendiary bombs burned all night. S/L McNab took to the air [alone] and encountered eight or nine ME-109s, shooting one down. This was assessed as probably destroyed. F/O Hyde returned from hospital and proceeded to Sir Courtauld Thompson's house to convalesce. Enemy aircraft were overhead most of the night. Three or four bombs were dropped near the station at 4 a.m.

September 8   F/L McGregor amongst other complaints had a pain across his chest, generally diagnosed in the absence of the MO [medical officer] as indigestion. Latter returned in the evening slightly AWOL [absent without leave] and other things. F/O Briese retained horseshoe championship during most of the afternoon.

September 9   The Squadron was scrambled to intercept enemy bombers. While climbing to manoeuvre for position of advantage, a protective screen of ME-109s was encountered above and proceeding south. These a/c attacked the Squadron and F/O W.B.M. Millar was shot down. He baled out but was found to be wounded in the leg and to have sustained burns. We managed to add an ME-109 to the list of destroyed, F/O Peterson blowing one to bits, and three ME-109s were severely damaged, two by F/O P.W. Lochnan and one by S/L McNab. The night was quiet around the station, a few bombs being heard dropping in London. Twenty-four-hour leaves are not being spent in London as frequently as heretofore for some reason.

September 11   [Senior officers] from headquarters came out to pay a visit. As usual when we have a gallery a flap started and the Squadron scrambled in their best fashion and came back an hour later with a mixed bag to lay at the Air Officer Commanding's feet. F/L McGregor and F/O

Molson shot down one HE-111 each. S/L McNab and F/O Christmas damaged one HE-111 each. F/O Yuile destroyed one JU-52. F/O Little was shot down. He managed to bale out but was wounded in the leg and was taken to hospital. F/O Lochnan crash-landed near Romney due to enemy action.

By night there were the usual pyrotechnics in the sky from the a/a, one cartridge case coming down near the mess, misidentified as ten whistling bombs and causing a premium for space under the beds in one room. The adjutant and F/L McGregor had dinner together fairly amicably on both sides. It is thought the adjutant was just too tired after a night in the Hungaria Restaurant or somewhere.

September 12 The Squadron was visited by the Honorable Harold Balfour, MC, Parliamentary Under Secretary of State for Air, who gave an account of the progress of the Joint Air Training Plan in Canada. It appears that the Empire Scheme is plodding along in a fashion that is very satisfactory to everybody, including the Germans no doubt, in that after sixteen months travail, the scheme will produce some pilots to be sent over here next January. They may surprise everybody by sending along a handful in November who will most probably be chosen reading from the bottom of the class. Considering that it takes an elephant twenty months to produce an offspring, this is considered a good show by all.

September 14 Some subsections were sent up in the morning to investigate this or patrol that. The day started off rather badly for F/O Molson who drew the dawn met [weather] flight while the rest of the pilots were sleeping peacefully.

September 15 This Sunday was a day of great activity, keeping the Squadron at readiness practically all day. The first scramble found the Squadron engaging the enemy to disadvantage as they came out of the sun from above, S/L

McNab and F/O Nesbitt being the only two pilots to engage. F/O Nesbitt destroyed one ME-109 but was himself shot down, escaping by parachute. He was found to have injured his head and was placed in the hospital for observation. F/O Smither did not return from this action.

The Squadron again went into action with S/L McNab leading shortly after 1400 hours. South of London a formation of enemy bombers with fighter escort was intercepted. In the ensuing engagement one HE-111 was destroyed by S/L McNab and one destroyed, shared with 229 Squadron, by F/O Lochnan. Two HE-111s probably destroyed were credited to F/L McGregor and F/O Russel. F/O R.W. Norris got a probable ME-109 and S/L McNab and F/O Pitcher were each credited with a damaged HE-111. F/O Yuile was wounded in the shoulder but courageously brought his a/c home safely.

Ernie McNab, sometimes called The McNab, wrote an article for the *Rockcliffe Air Review* of May 1941, about this mass Sunday encounter, considered the turning point in the Battle of Britain, in which he said, "There must have been nearly a thousand aeroplanes milling in a small area just south of London. It was a quick shot and away for someone was sure to be on your own tail. In after fifteen minutes there was hardly a plane in the sky — the Germans had run for home."

September 16 The Squadron was scrambled but no e/a was sighted. London got another pasting according to the leave boys, who thought the rain might cause hostilities to cease and mistakenly spent the night in town. They are now completely cured.

September 18 Enemy aircraft were coming over in batches at 20,000 feet, making it difficult for us to engage. On one of these scrambles F/O E.W. Beardmore, who became detached from the Squadron and joined up with 229 Squadron, was forced to take to his parachute, landing near shore in the Thames. He sustained slight injuries. The Navy returned him to us battered and bloodied but in very prime condition on the whole. Air-raid warnings were continuous all day. One attack on the station occurred. The civilians in the neighborhood must have spent the day running in and out of the shelters as the sirens were so busy that one never knew whether it was the alarm or the all-clear. The first evidence of red tape reminiscent of Canada appeared at this station today, which has been singularly free of that sort of stuff up till now. Scarves and sweaters will not be tolerated in future in place of collars and ties. Apparently when called from 30 minutes available to immediate readiness and expected to be airborne in no time at all, the pilots will have to be inspected and passed as neat and tidy to go up and engage the King's enemies.

The usual bangs and crashes were heard [during] the night but the vicinity looked much the same in the morning.

September 19 F/Os Beardmore and Nesbitt at Taplow and Desloges, Little and Millar at Bramshot, all wounded, are progressing favorably. F/L Corbett visited the Squadron on his way to convalesce in Wales. F/O R. Smither was buried today. S/L McNab and F/Os Pitcher, Russel and Briese attended the funeral, representing the Squadron.

September 20 F/L Alex Kentski, ex-Canadian and now with the Polska Escadra [Polish Squadron], entertained before dinner with an impromtu sleight-of-hand show and a certain amount of acrobatics which baffled the onlookers completely.

September 21 At 1800 hours a wing formation [three squadrons, twelve Hurricanes each] from the station took off to intercept. There was some doubt among the three squadrons as to which squadron was to lead and all took off together, fortunately without accident. No spectators could be found who could give an eyewitness account as they had their eyes closed, fingers crossed and were completely demoralized. The teams lined up, with the Polska Escadra and No. 1

defending the west end, and No. 229 the east. At a given signal from the controller, or a German spy, the opposing a/c advanced toward each other at the greatest possible speed, but the decision, a close one, must go to 229 Squadron who made up their minds first and passed over the heads of our boys, clearing them easily by about two feet. The matter straightened itself out in the air, however, but no interception was made, although e/a were seen a long way off the coast. This was the first wing formation operational flight from Northolt.

September 22   The state of the services was advanced from Alert 2 to Alert 1 as invasion is considered imminent. The Air Officer Commanding had tea at dispersal with the Squadron.

September 23   Many sissy ME-109s were sighted at considerable height above us but we could not reach them and they did not come down to play. The usual night bombing went on.

September 24   F/O Desloges received his flight lieutenant's stripes today but of course was not present to celebrate. Heavy bombing all night occurred in the vicinity of the Orchard, the favorite pub, endangering the lives of a great percentage of our pilots from being trampled to death in the rush for cover — that is, those that were able to locomote.

September 25   F/Os Peterson and Russel were dispatched to intercept some single e/a. A DO-215 was sighted and duly engaged, the Observer Corps afterward confirming that it had fallen into the sea near Worthing. Air Marshal W.A. Bishop, VC, DSO, MC, DFC, accompanied by the Air Officer Commanding, visited the Squadron during the afternoon and the movie camera people had a field day. In the evening e/a dropped bombs in the vicinity of the aerodrome and quarters, two of the barracks actually receiving hits but no casualties resulted.

September 26 The King paid a visit to Northolt and came down to our dispersal. All officers present lined up and the King shook hands with each one and spoke a few words. He congratulated the Squadron on their work and took a keen interest in the proceedings. Viscount Gort was also on the station in the morning. The CO [McNab] had a chatter with him and was not particularly impressed. There is an epidemic of colds about and F/L Reyno and F/O Briese went sick today.

September 27 The Squadron sighted a formation of thirty JU-88s escorted by ME-110s and 109s and went into the attack with the following results: one JU-88 destroyed by Blue Section, S/L McNab, F/Os E. de P. Brown and Christmas; one JU-88 probably destroyed, F/L McGregor; four ME-110s destroyed, one by S/L McNab and one by F/O Lochnan shared with 303 Squadron. Two were destroyed by F/O Russel, one of these being shared with 303. One ME-109 destroyed by F/O Russel. One ME-110 damaged by F/O Norris. F/Os Lochnan and Sprenger had their a/c shot up and made safe forced landings. F/O Peterson was missing and it was later discovered that he had been killed in the engagement.

In the second encounter with the enemy at noon, the Squadron could muster only eight planes but were accompanied by 229 Squadron. About twenty ME-109s were sighted near Gatwick about 2,000 feet above the Squadron. They attacked out of the sun but we had no casualties and F/L McGregor was able to damage one before they could make good their escape.

Around three o'clock in the afternoon the Squadron was again scrambled with 229 Squadron. Only six aircraft of our Squadron took part in this engagement as the two previous patrols had taken heavy toll of a/c serviceability. South of London fifteen or twenty DO-215s escorted by fighters were intercepted and five of the Dorniers were destroyed and one damaged. One was credited to F/O Brown and the other four were shared with 229 Squadron by

F/L McGregor, F/O Pitcher, F/O Yuile and F/O Russel. We had no casualties.

By the end of the day the Squadron was a very tired, unshaven group of warriors. They are so tired that they immediately drop asleep, not hearing or caring about the funny noises that go on in the neighborhood. Operating as a wing creates quite a bit of confusion as regards enemy casualties in that pilots team up with other friendly fighters to do the necessary and the reports have to be very carefully sifted out to get the correct assessment. First reports this morning indicated eight JU-88s destroyed but a short and to-the-point explanation by the CO said that everybody had taken a poke at the same machine, which isn't exactly cricket, or good tactics.

Later, despite the success of the 27th against the DO-215, the diary noted, "These babies seem pretty tough as every time we run into them we fill them full of lead but cannot claim anything much more than damaged."

Combat reports were filed after every action. They were not usually written into the squadron diary but were attached to it. Here are a couple of examples from the action of September 27:

> S/L McNab: I was leading two squadrons, No. 1 Canadian and 303. Gathered section together after attack on bomber and climbed to 18,000 feet where twenty-plus ME-110s were in a defensive circle attacked by a number of Hurricanes. I noticed an ME-110 break circle and head for coast. In company with another Hurricane (squadron unknown) attacked and finally ME-110 showed flame along port side, turned onto its back and crashed in flames.

> F/O Russel: I was flying Green 3 when we sighted bombers and was attacked by one ME-110 from the starboard beam. In dodging out of his way, I joined with three 109s flying in line astern. I gave No. 3 about three seconds burst and he fell off to the left and baled

out; as he was doing so, I could not see any material damage although my burst must have hit him as I was directly beneath him and about seventy yards behind him when I fired. In my breakaway, I lost considerable height and I was successful in joining with leader [McNab]. We climbed to attack ME-110s which were flying in a defensive circle over Biggin Hill area. We attacked from northeast against the circle. I got separated in this attack and attacked a smaller group, which were slightly lower to the south. I attacked an ME-110 from slightly above and behind in a tight turn, gave him about eight seconds burst which started the port engine on fire. He fell away and about four Hurricanes set on him and he crashed somewhere in the vicinity of East Grinstead. At this point another ME-110 broke away and about four of us set on it. He crashed about ten miles south of my first one in a clearing between a lot of trees. My first landed in a field behind quite a big house near a small town with a cement road running in front.

Squadrons usually flew in sections of three aircraft each. The sections were distinguished by a color, usually red, blue, green and yellow for a twelve-plane squadron. The section leader was No. 1, his right-hand man No. 2 and his left-hand pilot No. 3. Sections of four planes were also used.

September 28 The night was made hideous with loud bangs.

September 29 A day of patrols being vectored all over the place. F/L McGregor became progressively bitter against the controller. However, he, or rather, they, do not mend their ways and the number of wasted miles that are flown if added together, placed end to end, would stretch from here to dear old Montreal, or to whatever dear old place one belongs to.

The padre held a short service in the afternoon which was well attended and later accompanied some of the

Squadron to Uxbridge for a steak dinner. The place was crowded and the advance guard, F/O Pitcher, had neglected to do his duty to order a table. The Squadron song was rendered to the assembled multitude by a quartet which did not exactly bring down the house, but passed off without incident.

September 30 In the late afternoon contact was made with ME-109s escorting enemy bombers and F/L McGregor shot down an ME-109 and F/O Brown damaged another but his a/c was in turn damaged and he nosed up on landing at base. Air Marshal Bishop paid a visit to the Squadron at tea time. Bombing was carried out in the district by single raiders all night.

October 1 F/Os Nesbitt and Beardmore were back with the Squadron today for the first time since their parachute jumps. There is a decided shortage of pilots at the moment as the CO, F/L Reyno, and F/Os Briese, Brown and Norris are in hospital with colds.

October 2 F/O Hyde reported for duty today, having fully recovered from his burns and parachute jump.

October 3 Capt. R.J. Nodwell, Royal Canadian Army Medical Corps, joined the Squadron to replace Capt. W.D. Rankin who is at Taplow [Hospital] with pneumonia. This is the first real solid day of rain with fog that we have had since we became operational on August 17th and it was very welcome.

October 4 We received word today that the CO has been awarded the DFC [Distinguished Flying Cross]. The Squadron was released an hour earlier than usual and rejoicing was general.

October 5 Three patrols were carried out in wing formation. In the first contact, made with about sixty ME-109s and fifteen ME-110s, considerable milling about resulted. F/O Molson was wounded and baled out, doing a delayed jump. He was amply revenged as the Squadron bag for the fight was three ME-109s destroyed [by McGregor, Pitcher and Christmas], one ME-109 damaged and two ME-110s damaged.

October 6 At approximately 1315 hours a single raider came out of cloud at about 300 feet and dropped a 1,000-pound bomb between the hangars and a delayed-action bomb close beside it. The 1,000-pounder did some damage to both hangars, smashed up two Hurricanes and killed a sergeant-pilot of 303 Squadron and one of the station defence airmen. The station defence were unable to get a crack at the marauder as no one had told them that the raider was coming, or their guns were not loaded, or the corporal wasn't there to give the order to fire, or something. Words stronger than "a poor show" are required here to describe our reception to this marauder and here they are — it was a God damn bloody awful balls-up. This is the first time that profanity has crept into these pages and it is believed that all will be forgiven by the reader if he was present, but, anyway, apologies to the padre and any others who object.

October 7 Although many ME-109s were seen, only one contact was made with the enemy. On this occasion F/O Lochnan was credited with one ME-109 destroyed but F/O Nesbitt had his a/c severely damaged and landed at Biggin Hill.

Capt. Nodwell, the medical officer, reported to his superiors on this date that the pilots of No. 1 Squadron had had no leave since arrival in England in June. He added: "There is a definite air of constant tension and they are unable to relax as they are practically on constant call. The pilots go to work with forced enthusiasm and appear to be suffering from strain and general tiredness."

October 8 Word was received that F/L Gordon McGregor and F/O Dal Russel have been awarded the DFC. Later in the day a signal informed us that we are to be moved to Prestwick as soon as 615 Squadron arrives here to relieve us.

October 10 615 Squadron arrived on the station in the forenoon and preparations were immediately made for the Squadron to take off for Prestwick. Seventeen a/c took off at 1400 hours, leaving the CO and F/O Pitcher, still grounded by colds, to travel by car with the intelligence officer. The adjutant, medical officer and dental officer departed by rail. The Squadron made two stops en route owing to weather and landed at Catterick about four in the afternoon where we spent the night.

Thus ended No. 1's front-line action in the Battle of Britain. The Squadron, first in the RCAF to see combat, entered the battle August 17, 1940, made its first kill August 26, and by the time it was pulled out October 9 had destroyed thirty German planes, probably destroyed eight and damaged thirty-five. Three pilots were killed (F/O R.L Edwards, F/O R. Smither and F/O O.J. Peterson) and ten others wounded, mainly by flames in the cockpit. The ground crew kept the Hurricanes flying three or four patrols a day. Fitters worked on the engines, riggers on the airframes and the armorers cleaned eight Browning machine-guns, often still warm from firing, and reloaded the ammunition boxes.

PRESTWICK, SCOTLAND

October 11 An uneventful flight was made to Prestwick where the quarters were found to be comfortable and the food excellent. It is hoped that our record of bringing the Hun after us every station we settle at will be broken. Middle Wallop, Croydon and Northolt all received their first bombing while we were there and it would be a shame to have the peaceful surroundings of this station broken.

October 12 The first convoy arrived today, parts of it in somewhat battered condition. The bus had made an unsuccessful attempt to pass under a low bridge but there were no serious casualties. The tires had to be deflated before the bus could be unstuck. As we were not to become operational till dawn Sunday, most pilots took the opportunity to investigate the countryside and its inhabitants. Both are thoroughly satisfactory. The war seems very far away.

October 13 Operational flying commenced at dawn with one section at readiness and two at fifteen-minutes available. This state is maintained during the day and a dusk patrol of one section was carried out over the Clyde area.

October 15 Leave for the men commenced, seven days being granted to sixty-nine in the first batch. As there were no funds available it speaks very highly of our pay lieutenant Hall that he managed an overdraft to look after the boys till funds arrive from London.

October 16 An inspection of the camp blackout disclosed many uncovered lights. It really needs a few bombs to be dropped in the vicinity before a blackout is taken seriously.

October 17 Orders were received for the Squadron to patrol tomorrow an armed merchant cruiser up the coast, one section relieving another so that cover would be provided all day. This is the first convoy work that we have had.

October 18 Heavy fog prevented cover being provided for the armed merchant vessel, which reached port without our assistance. Periodically, ops over at Turnhouse send through a signal to "be on our toes," but so far this has not developed any further. It is believed that this is done merely to remind us that we are still operational and that the war still goes on.

October 20 It being the late closing night in this country [Scotland], most of the pilots took advantage of it at the very convenient pub next door, The Orange Field.

October 21 The billeting problem is acute in this district as the mess is full of Canadians, Poles and Indians, and all available hotels and rooms in Prestwick are jammed with the overflow from the station as well as evacuees from the south. The Indians are a very nice type, well turned out, some with turbans and beards and others without, speaking perfect Oxford English. But they constitute quite a problem as far as messing is concerned. Different religions compel varied diets. There are also the troubles with pay and allowances, as some boast of six wives. These are looked on with envy by some of the more virile pilots and with awe by the older ones.

October 24 CBC radio experts made a recording of our messages home which is to be broadcast on Monday night. The cable office did quite a business advising those who are interested to listen in at that time.

October 25 The CO, intelligence officer and adjutant nearly attended the wrong dinner in Glasgow. It appears that the adjutant thought the invitation had come from the district commissioner, but on arrival at the rendezvous, the Central Hotel, it was discovered that there isn't any such animal. However, on the noticeboard there was a gent named Sir Horace Bilsland entertaining, so it was decided he must be the host. Luckily, before the butler announced the names the CO smelt a rat, and further investigation disclosed that the invitation came from the Honorable James G. Gardiner, Minister of War Services at home. He is a native of a place called Regina but nevertheless had ordered a very good meal with refreshments at suitable intervals. [The CO, McNab, came from Regina.]

October 26 The Air Officer Commanding, Air Commodore Saul, came and went, leaving a badly shattered Squadron. Everything went wrong, everything we did is wrong, the errors of omission and commission were discussed in no uncertain terms, we evidently don't know a war is on, etc., etc. He left for Glasgow by road, taking the CO with him, and eventually sent back for their overnight kit, so things must be getting patched up.

October 27 The AOC arrived back with the CO and was in a better frame of mind, although we were unable to lay out a red carpet for him to keep his tootsies from getting muddy. A hockey practice was held in the rink at Ayr. There was a noticeable lack of condition.

October 30 An engineer of the Rolls-Royce Company gave pilots a lecture on the Merlin engine and how to treat it to ensure maximum performance and life, the latter somewhat dependent on the aim of the Jerries. The adjutant's room had to be evacuated while smoke [from a faulty stove] cleared out, this stopping the war for about half an hour.

October 31 The readiness section was ordered to escort an aircraft carrier until dusk. This duty carried the section some distance from base and R/T [radio-telephone] touch was lost. Control received word that the a/c carrier was being attacked and the first section shot down and a second section was ordered to their assistance. This section found the carrier and the first section intact and all six a/c returned to base at dusk without having sighted any e/a.

November 1 The mess dance was a great success, the free refreshments possibly having something to do with it, and everybody enjoyed it except F/O Russel, who was grossly exploited. It appears that as the taxi drove off, having been paid in advance to take his guest home, a brother officer stepped in on the other side and had the pleasure of escorting the lady home at F/O Russel's expense, a very neat piece of timing, or two-timing as the aggrieved party asserts.

November 2 S/L McGregor was posted in orders as Officer Commanding the Squadron vice W/C McNab. At 2 p.m. a heavy downpour with high winds started. Seeing the men go round [wrapped in] ground sheets only made one wish that the man who gave the order to leave our slickers behind in Halifax should be with us and put on guard duty in one of these downpours with only the sheet to protect him.

November 8 In the evening a hockey team composed of Squadron personnel and billed as Les Canadiens for advertisement purposes played against the Ayr Raiders in the local hockey stadium. Our opponents were all Canadian hockey players who had been brought to this country some years ago to play for the town and we were rather embarrassed by the thought that we would be greatly outclassed. However, after securing a lead of seven goals to one, the Ayr Raiders lifted the pressure in order to make the game interesting, and the final score amounted to 10 to 6.

November 9 F/L E.W. Beardmore [posted back to Canada] was in ripe condition by the time he left [for the train]. The baggage was duly chalked with obscene remarks. We wonder how long it will be before Beardmore will remove the pair of silk scanties which were left hanging out of one of his trunks.

November 11 In the evening a cocktail party and farewell dinner was held in honor of W/C McNab, who leaves the Squadron tomorrow to take over duties with the RAF. F/O Nesbitt broke precedent and proposed a toast to the King prematurely so that he could have a smoke.

November 16 The Saturday night dance at the Marine found nearly all pilots in attendance, with friends, and there was the usual difficulty with the bar, getting drinks when you wanted them without being knocked down and trampled on.

November 17 In the evening a hockey game between the officers and men resulted in a victory for the latter, 6 to 4. The officers were handicapped by having only two substitutes while their opponents had three complete forward lines.

November 18 The CO [S/L McGregor] tried to get a practice homing from Turnhouse but apparently Bloodhound, which is the call name for the controller, had lost the scent, making a guess after sixteen minutes which would have landed the section far, far away from home. A letter is being dispatched on the subject.

November 21 Winds of gale force and the soggy condition of the field limited flying and routine flights were cancelled. The station showed a movie of the methods employed by the Germans to extract information from prisoners. Some mess bills are apt to be high this month, as doors are rather expensive items to be replaced.

November 22 As most of the Indian pilots were leaving in the morning, they did some entertaining before, during and after dinner. Later a dance at The Orange Field was attended by many of the pilots, but there was a certain amount of unpleasantness with the management over the breaking of their glasses.

November 24 Seventeen large cases of stores arrived from Ottawa for the Squadron and were found to contain bits and pieces for a Lysander [aircraft].

November 26 Weather closed in. F/O Bill Sprenger was unable to keep in touch with R/T and crashed out of cloud with 700-foot ceiling on the west side of Loch Lomond, causing his instantaneous death. Great guy, Bill.

November 28 F/O Sprenger's funeral at Alexandria was attended by the CO and all officers not on readiness. Detachments also attended from the Royal Artillery, the Alexandria Firemen and one unit of women, F/O Sprenger being buried in a very pretty cemetery in sight of Loch Lomond where he met his death.

Mr. Ralston [Col. J.L. Ralston, Minister of National Defence] and Col. McGee met officers of the Squadron in Glasgow and entertained them. These gentlemen had just arrived in Glasgow from Canada by boat half an hour previously. Col. Ralston was in a receptive frame of mind, notwithstanding a severe attack of sciatica, but the time was too short to tell him all our ideas about No. 1 Squadron, the Empire Training Scheme and generally how the war should be run.

November 29 This is St. Andrew's Day, and most of the officers participated in some function, either at a dinner or at a dance. The adjutant [attended] a dinner of the Royal Scots Fusiliers, complete with haggis, pipers, band and ambrosia, was inveigled into a form of sport called "Are you there, Moriarty?" and damned near had his can beaten off.

The acute mail shortage which everybody has experienced for the past two or three weeks was solved by a footnote in headquarters orders stating that mail posted in Canada between the 17th and 23rd of last month had all been lost through enemy action at sea.

December 5 Sir Harry Lauder [Scottish entertainer] visited the Squadron in the evening and put on an act in conjunction with the concert party in the YM.

December 6 Late at night, the CO was advised that the Squadron was moving to Wick. The news was not believed by most.

December 7 The news was almost right. The new home of the Squadron is to be Castletown, the most northerly point in Scotland and near Wick. It is believed that the powers-that-be [thought] that the Canadians are used to winter weather and should be stationed at this spot. F/Ls Reyno and Corbett are going to 112 Squadron to start No. 2 Canadian Squadron, and so we start to break up.

December 8 Eighteen a/c departed for Castletown at 0945 hours. An air party of eighteen men and urgently needed equipment departed for Castletown in two Bombay a/c at 1030 hours. Main party departed by train at 1845 hours.

CASTLETOWN, SCOTLAND

December 9 The accommodation is strained to the utmost with the addition of half of our Squadron. Officers are billeted in the Royal Hotel, Thurso, eight miles from the aerodrome. The airmen are stationed on the aerodrome in huts. All accommodation is very cold and not good. Thurso is a very small village with little entertainment, few women and the coldest hotel rooms ever experienced. Dispersal is in an old dilapidated farmhouse. It is dark until 0915 hours, and the sun goes down about 1530 hours and never gets very high up in the sky.

The convoy encountered very mountainous country with sharp turns and narrow roads. Snow and ice made progress very slow and dangerous. One jeep did not make a turn in the road over a bridge the other side of Inverness and crashed down the cutting onto a railway track, catching fire just when the Scottish Express was due. The driver was pulled out, the fire put out and the train stopped within a few minutes. The driver was sent to hospital with a broken wrist and possible fracture of the skull, which was really very little when one considers the shape of the jeep. [There were] many deer on the way through the hills, some being so close that you could hit them over the head with a stick.

December 10 Telephone communication on the station is bad and great difficulty is encountered in endeavoring to get all personnel settled due to large distances between various parts of the Squadron. [The medical officer reported: "The airmen's mess is in a filthy condition. The floor is covered by a mucky layer of dirt which is a mixture of dirt tracked in from outside, wash water and food. The hall has a rancid odor."]

December 13 It was decided to take over an army camp composed of twenty-eight Nissen huts for the Squadron, known as the Thurso Castle Camp, distant eight miles from the aerodrome. It is keenly felt here that this station will receive considerable attention during any invasion because of the proximity of the fleet [at Scapa Flow], which the station is to protect from any bombing raids.

December 14 F/L Paul Pitcher took over command of the Squadron from S/L McGregor. Most of the day was spent trying to get beds, blankets, etc. for the airmen in Thurso Castle Camp. There is no water in the camp, which makes it very difficult to cook, etc. All cooking is being done by our own cooks on a portable cooker. Meals are very good. Great scarcity of coal in the camp.

December 15 Great difficulty encountered in endeavoring to arrange transport to move 200 men a distance of eight miles four times a day as well as thirty-two officers four or five times each day, rations, coal and store runs being additional. Our old CO, S/L McGregor, threw a farewell cocktail party and with a slight intermission for dinner the party continued till about 0230 hours. It's a good thing we are not losing our COs every day.

December 17 A number of scrambles occurred during the day, one section being vectored to the northern part of the Orkneys, but no e/a were sighted.

December 20 Daylight period is short and hard to get enough practice flying.

December 21 Large Christmas mails arrived from Canada, taking six days to come from London. A present was received for £22 from the Canadian Red Cross to be used for Christmas dinners for the airmen.

December 22 F/O Hyde searched the surrounding country and finally located the only Christmas tree in the district. One of the readiness section had to arrange for a stand-in as his teeth disappeared down the drainpipe in his basin when retiring last night, but were subsequently rescued and became serviceable with their owner later in the day. The CO and a party found a pub at Betty Hills about thirty miles west of this place, with a very hospitable host who has not had a guest for at least eighteen months but who has got some very nice stuff called Old Grouse that will keep the cold out.

December 23 Some Christmas and New Year's leave was given to a few personnel who could be spared.

December 24 There was one scramble during the day with nothing to report. Some practice flying was carried out by two sections. A Christmas dinner was held for the men, all arrangements being well provided for under the direction of F/L Cockram [padre] and F/Os Hyde and Brown. The officers served the men their dinner and were unable to get any for themselves. All personnel seemed to enjoy the entertainment. The meal consisted of tomato soup, turkey and plum pudding with the usual trimmings, and fruit and nuts and afterwards beer with a present for each man from the Y. Considering the inexperience of the waiters, a fair job was done.

December 25 Christmas Eve being what it was, today was spent recuperating. Those not actually on duty were released. Some training was proceeded with, both in the morning and afternoon, and the evening patrol went out. During the night we had a local Lady Godiva, without her horse, wandering around our rooms at the hotel, to the embarrassment of our pilots — she was just a little too plastered to be of any use to anybody.

December 26 An inspection was made of the hotel at John O'Groats and it was found to be in the same state as all inns in the restricted area, very old and dismal and no guests.

December 27 F/O Hanbury reports that Aberdeen is a good place for an evening, and looked it.

December 28 F/L Nesbitt received a cable announcing the birth of a son on the 19th, to be known as Caithness Thurso Nesbitt, or Thirsty for short, after his old man.

December 29 Baths were arranged for the airmen about sixteen miles from the station. This was their first opportunity for a bath for twenty-one days. F/Os Boomer and Norris ran out of petrol [on return from a long sea patrol in bad weather] and crash-landed. F/O Boomer hit obstruction poles [to prevent German landings] and damaged his a/c and his person. F/O Norris somehow landed between these poles in heavy mud with wheels down and no damage. F/Os Briese, Fumerton and Connell returned [from a shoot] with two deer, one fox and about twenty hares destroyed.

[The deer] have been handed over to the hotel chef for our future use.

December 31 The station cocktail party was a great success if numbers count for anything. Our transport suffered rather heavily from the slippery roads and other complications peculiar to this particular evening.

1941

THE WAR BECAME WORLD-WIDE in 1941. Germany attacked Russia and Japan attacked the United States. Britain tried to regroup after the disastrous withdrawal of its army from defeated France in 1940, continued air assaults on its cities and losses in North Africa. Canada's armed forces expanded rapidly. The RCAF mounted its first offensive operation over enemy territory on April 15 with a fighter sweep led by W/C Gordon McGregor, formerly of No. 1 Squadron. RCAF bombers made their first strike at Germany June 12. No. 1 Squadron opened the year in the snows of northeast Scotland, moved down the east coast in early spring and went on to Biggin Hill, near London, in the fall.

CASTLETOWN, SCOTLAND

January 1 A bit more snow fell during the night and it would be a grand New Year's Day in any other place, preferably Canada.

January 3 A lecture on gas, and the nasty things it does to you, was given by F/O Biggs. The places on one's person that a certain kind of gas attacks first were closely noted by the pilots.

January 4 We discovered a navigator's school at Dyce, flying Whitleys, who are agreeable to calling for any of our officers who are going on leave and taking them as far south as possible. This will be very useful as the train trip to Inverness has to be experienced to be believed.

January 9 Tables arrived for the airmen's mess, making it no longer necessary for them to hold their plates in their hands when eating their meals. These tables were on order for eighteen weeks.

January 11 The Duke of Sutherland extended a kind invitation to our officers to shoot over his estate. The pay [officer] and the DO [dental officer] had some revolver practice in preparation for the coming invasion, and any Jerries in their vicinity may get frightened, but not shot.

January 14   The [visiting Canadian] Chief of Air Staff went over everything with a fine-tooth comb, even going into the question of typewriters with the adjutant, and it is now believed that instead of getting more we will lose one.

January 15   The CO was right on his toes at an early hour this morning with the remark that life up here was composed of wine, sleep and song.

January 16   The road to Thurso being blocked [by snow and abandoned vehicles, including an ambulance], it took approximately two hours to get all the personnel back to camp. Our transport [jeeps] were the only vehicles which could negotiate the road, enabling the Squadron to remain operational when the other squadrons were unserviceable.

January 18   Heavy blizzard prevented any operational flying. An enemy aircraft circled the aerodrome but could not be seen. This a/c was obviously lost.

January 22   Train communication is now cut off and the only road open is the one between Thurso and Castletown, due to our motor transport. There are only seven of the original officers remaining in the Squadron of the twenty-six that arrived from Canada seven months ago.

January 26   A rum issue was arranged and greatly appreciated by the men who were working in the open all day. It was real Navy rum, which hit the right spot.

January 29   There are about twenty officers and airmen scattered from Edinburgh to Castletown trying to get back to the Squadron, and short of funds by the phone calls that come through.

January 30 Colds and influenza prevalent in Squadron.

January 31 S/L Pitcher [commanding officer] confined to quarters with measles.

February 2 S/L Pitcher removed from Royal Hotel, Thurso, to hospital in Wick. A few officers attended a cocktail party at 260 Squadron. The drive home with acting CO F/L Christmas at the wheel was made in low gear successfully, which tells the story of the party fully.

February 6 F/L Jack Morrison was married to Miss Stephanie Wood. Eleven o'clock was zero hour and he went quietly. There was no padre available so the job was done at the local JP's and in much quicker time than it takes a section of A flight to take off on a scramble. A reception was held at the bride's home with all the available officers present. F/L C.W. Trevena was best man and a cigarette box was presented from the officers.

February 7 The CO was visited in hospital at Wick. It is not recommended for anyone to get sick up here. He is quartered in a large, cold, bleak room with about twenty-five beds in it but no occupants and a very small fireplace. The food is none too good and nursing service rather limited and poor. However, the measles have subsided. The CO pleaded with tears in his eyes for someone to get him out of the hell-hole, but that is a matter for the MO.

February 11 Main party departed Castletown for Driffield [Yorkshire] by train, 185 ORs and 4 officers. An impromptu crap game on the station platform on a blanket resulted in filling the pockets of the acting CO.

DRIFFIELD, ENGLAND

February 15 Most of the day was taken up in getting the personnel settled in their quarters and unpacking our equipment preparatory to becoming again operational. Good accommodation and food.

February 17 A warning movement order was received today. It indicated that the Squadron was to move to Digby [Lincolnshire] on February 28, disturbing our routine again before we are really settled in this station. We feel like a group of tourists. Hull was the centre of attraction in the evening and we hear that the hunting season is in full swing. We should like to warn one and all concerning a certain little item [venereal disease] which, if contracted, means a loss of pay. Hull has won the national record of being the worst place in England for this charming game.

February 18 We regret to report that the Squadron lost a very swell guy this morning. A section of two was scrambled. F/L J.B. Reynolds failed to return. Later advice confirmed his death at Bridlington, Yorkshire, due to a flying accident. It was just one of those things that will never be known.

February 21 One section was scrambled and was vectored onto a Blenheim a/c who would not give the letters of the day [recognition signal]. F/O Wallace put a burst across his bow and he quickly identified himself as a friendly a/c.

February 22 The CO, F/Ls Norris, Nesbitt, Morrison, Johnstone and Watson and F/Os Biggs and Neal departed this station to attend the funeral of F/L Reynolds at Digby. The funeral party was composed of a firing and bearer party supplied from this Squadron and an escort party kindly supplied by No. 2 Canadian Squadron at Digby.

February 25 Hull again received the Squadron's attentions with no casualties as of yet.

February 28 Squadron flew to Digby, departing Driffield at 1430 hours. Main party departed by convoy at 1500.

DIGBY, ENGLAND

March 1 Squadron number changed from No. 1 Canadian Squadron to 401 Squadron, RCAF. [The RAF assigned RCAF squadrons numbers in the 400 series to avoid confusion with its own units. Canada was given no say in the numbering of its squadrons.]

March 4 In Lincoln in the evening there was a certain amount of competition for a blonde, but this died out when she opened her mouth and exhibited great gaps in her pearlies. At any rate there would have been no evidence of tooth marks, but even this was not sufficient lure.

March 6 F/L Morrison had his first anniversary — one month — and it was duly celebrated by some of his friends with rum and champagne.

March 7 At 1230 hours during an air-raid warning an e/a machine-gunned and dropped five bombs of 250 pounds each, one of which was a time bomb. LAC Walker was confined to sick quarters due to shock from the bombing. One unexploded bomb was fired by the bomb disposal squad at 1400 hours. There were some muddy uniforms [but] damage was negligible, only a few windows knocked out of one hangar.

March 8 S/L Pitcher [is] en route to No. 1 Canadian General Hospital, having finally escaped from captivity in Wick. After getting over measles and near pneumonia, he had a go of scarlet fever, but he is now convalescent.

March 9 A lady announced as being from Regina stole the show [at a gala Squadron party] with her big black eyes, and gave people ideas, not that they didn't have them pretty well on tap before, but she just dangled everything before their eyes, which rather whets the appetite.

March 13 There seem to be regular nocturnal excursions into Lincoln to see "Three Guinea Gwen."

March 14 Movietown News once again came snooping around and all the young Casanovas did their best to unnoticeably thrust themselves into the foreground.

March 20 A lecture was given the pilots on ways and means of escaping, should any of them be unfortunate enough to become prisoners of war. One really needs to be a combination of miner, actor, linguist, thief and all-round tough guy to get away with it.

March 21 Two lots of movie people were around to get more shots as the ones they took the other day were blitzed in London.

March 25 F/O C.P. Henderson was killed when the aircraft he was testing crashed in flames about one mile from the aerodrome. A tough break for the Squadron.

March 28 Funeral of F/O Henderson was held in the afternoon and interment made in Digby Cemetery. The adjutant, or what was left of him, arrived back after three or four days' leave. Somebody or something with nails in it had done a wizard show on his puss, and by his general appearance he seems to have enjoyed his leave.

March 31 The month just completed has been a very active one. Eighty-four scrambles with a total of 148 operational hours; numerous practice flights totalling 667 hours. Officers 33, airmen 318.

April 3 It is to be hoped that we will soon be equipped with [new model Hurricanes] as the present mounts are pretty well obsolete. They did their job last fall but with the new and improved types Jerry now possesses they are out of the picture. Even our own bombers are reported by various pilots to have more speed, which is a poor state of affairs for our operational fighter Squadron.

It was a common complaint throughout the RCAF overseas that it was always the last among the Commonwealth and Allied air forces to get new equipment. The Canadian government never raised a whisper of protest, in contrast to the Australian government, for instance, which backed up its squadrons when they refused to fly old planes. RCAF Headquarters in London had no operational command and thus no say whatever in the disposition and use of Canadian squadrons, which received their orders daily from the RAF on what they were to do, and how to do it. RCAF Headquarters had charge of administration only and, as already noted, this did not even extend to numbering Canadian squadrons. The result was that Canadian units were constantly bombarded throughout the war with myriad questions about administrative details. Simple misspellings were often called to the attention of squadron commanders and adjutants, wasting time and paper.

April 5 S/L P.B. Pitcher was a visitor from his hospital near Birmingham, looking a little pale and worn, part of which is believed caused by a farewell party given him by the MOs last night. He hopes to get back to us again in about three weeks.

April 13 Easter Sunday was almost completely ruined as there were no eggs for breakfast. There was quite the largest turnout for church parade that there has been for some time, around seventy from this Squadron, with F/L Cockram giving his usual splendid sermon.

April 14   A Jerry took a crack at the place out of low cloud, dropping four bombs, three of which were 1,000-pounders, and the fourth very much smaller. [One] hit in the road, demolishing the post office and unfortunately causing two casualties in 402 Squadron, one being killed.

April 15   The Air Officer Commanding arrived on a visit and is still not satisfied with our monthly total of flying, or anything else for that matter, in his usual manner.

April 17   Reports of a heavy raid on London, they call it the heaviest since the war began, make one think twice before going down there on a forty-eight [forty-eight-hour leave].

April 18   F/L Watson returned from seven days' leave looking as if he needed another seven days to recuperate.

April 20   Both good and bad news was received today, the former being that the Squadron would be equipped with Hurricane IIs within a few days. The bad news was that compulsory PT [physical training] is about to be introduced by the station commander, as well as a monthly written exam on a/c recognition and allied subjects. Our CO won the first round about the PT as he advised the instructor that the only available time at the present is either 0415 hours or 2115, which foxed him temporarily, but the writing is on the wall, and soon there will be only the passive resistance that we can muster to this nuisance order.

The parachutes have had rubber dinghies attached to them, making the net weight somewhere just short of a ton, but will be useful for souvenirs after the war.

April 21   A draft of sixty-three [men] from Canada arrived, as usual completely without notice.

April 25   More nuisance regulations came into force in the mess. In future trousers are not be worn tucked into flying boots, but to be worn outside.

An early Second World War recruiting poster. "Adventure" was hardly the word for combat.

The basic fighter formation was three, or a "vic," for "V."

No. 1 Squadron, renumbered 401 in March 1941, had to fly the sluggish Hurricane until it received Spitfires in September 1941. The Canadians were always the last to get new planes and equipment because Canada held no operational air force command overseas.

Six Hurricanes of 401 Squadron on patrol over eastern England.

A rare occasion when the ground crew could work under cover.

The ground crew does an engine run-up on a Hurricane. Two men hold the tail down with their combined weight, one on each side of the fin, leaning into the prop-wash.

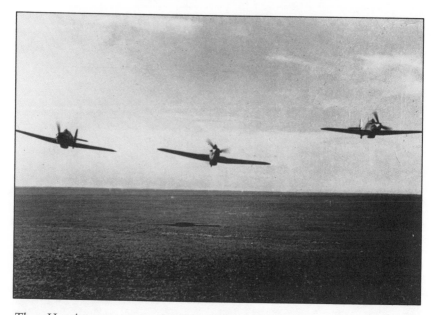

Three Hurricanes on a practice "beat-up." 401 Squadron when not engaged in aerial combat or escorting Allied bombers attacked ground targets, including launching sites of the German V 1, or buzz bomb.

Digging out from a snowstorm at Biggin Hill, near London, in February 1942.

April 27 About the only way one knows that Sunday has rolled around is to see the padre with his collar on backwards, as he appeared that way for breakfast today to advertise his church parade, which was well attended. The CO, S/L Dean Nesbitt, celebrated his promotion in the approved style, although the shortage of scotch makes it more difficult or less expensive than it was at Thurso. It cost him nine bottles up there, but only one tonight.

May 1 Some of the readiness pilots were awakened by their batmen and informed, much to their disgust, that as they were shortly to be at readiness, it might be a good idea to "get cracking." At that, no batman appeared on the casualty list. The MOs are having fun giving pilots tests for night flying vision, which consists of sitting in the absolute darkness for forty-five minutes and then showing a series of articles and letters which have to be identified. It is thought that if two or three only are correctly guessed, it will constitute a pass.

May 2 Five pilots who had gone down to Chilbolton to bring back our slightly moth-eaten [Hurricane] Mark IIs returned with them in the afternoon. It seems that these a/c have experienced a spot of trouble somewhere or other as some of them are "decorated" with holes made by cannon fire, which must have been repaired with tissue paper as it did not survive the return trip.

May 3 Our pilots took to night flying like a duck takes to water and are very keen on this type of flying. There were plenty of Jerries about and F/O Watson twice had one in his sights but was foiled by searchlights each time.

May 8 The Group Captain was up in one of our a/c and sat on the tail of a Jerry for some time but had nobody with him to tell him that the guns don't function very well when set at SAFE.

May 15 [On former adjutant F/L Norris being promoted to S/L:] It only goes to show that if one keeps on leave and out of people's mind and sight, the reward is bound to come sooner or later.

May 17 On an exhibition flight in connection with a War Weapons Week in a village near here, F/L George Hyde, one of the original No. 1 Canadian and lately of 402 Squadron, crashed and was instantaneously killed.

May 23 Another ex-member of 401 Squadron, F/O P.W. Lochnan, who joined us at Northolt, was killed with 400 Squadron. He volunteered for a sea rescue job in particularly dirty weather which caused the crash. Padre Cockram went down for the funeral [at Odiham] as well as F/Ls Morrison, Watson and Johnstone.

May 31 F/O Biggs [equipment officer] left for Canada this [Saturday] morning. During the drive down to London the MT driver broke all records, rules and regulations so that he could make the train connection to Liverpool. It was later learned (as usual) that he had until some time Monday to make it.

June 2 There was an unofficial party at the mess last night, attended by the padre and some people from ops. It was learned that the padre experienced some difficulty in parking his car.

June 8 Most of the pilots went over to Manby to look over the [German] HE-111 [bomber which had made a forced landing] and returned with most of it. An (almost) working model could have been assembled on the return trip in the bus.

June 10 The funeral took place today of LAC Lewis who died as a result of a motorcycle accident. The service was conducted by Padre Cockram.

June 17 The day broke bright and very hot and it came, as always, as a complete surprise as we are not accustomed to this sort of thing in this country. Mr. E.R. McEwan of the Canadian YMCA arrived to organize sports activities.

June 18 The Squadron, accompanied by 257 and 310 Squadrons, did a wing patrol over the Channel which lasted for about an hour and a half, and it was as hot as hell or hotter. The pilots reported that they had not seen any Jerries while over the No Man's Land of this war, and it appears that we will have to patrol the Unter der Linden in order to sight an honest-to-goodness Jerry.

June 19 The Honorable Vincent Massey [Canadian high commissioner in London] and Mrs. Massey visited the Squadron and had tea at Wellingore Grange [a satellite field].

June 20 It is just a year ago today that the Squadron disembarked at Liverpool and the occasion was duly celebrated with a dinner at Digby for the airmen of 401 and 402 Squadrons. The padre, F/L Cockram, did a great job as MC and there was an excellent floor show plus a bang-up orchestra. Oh yes! there was also a glorious repast and plenty of beer.

June 21 The officers held a dance at Ashby Hall. Some of our distinguished alumni came from distant parts, including F/Ls Christmas and Trevena from 403 and F/L Hillock and F/Os Fumerton and Mitchell from 406. Headquarters sent a large delegation of about six or eight, which is about six or eight more than they can possibly dispense with in London for a funeral. S/L Norris certainly put on a good show, bars all over the place, beautiful women and even a gondola in the pond. Through some slip-up drinks were on the house. The deficit is understood to be £133, quite a hefty sum. As 402 were on in the morning, there were no worries about early morning readiness or hangovers, so everybody could go full out, and did.

June 22 Bodies were littered all over the shambles that was our home, as beds were given up willingly for our guests, but around noon everything was cleaned up again and the place looked normal, if not the inmates. Hangovers were in the majority and there was a big run on the ice-cold drinks. It was a relief when the day was over. A lecture on the properties and use of rubber will have to be arranged. One pilot at the dance hall expected a certain manufactured article grew on trees in the park, as he came without and evidently tried to borrow some unsuccessfully.

June 23 The WAAFs had their dance tonight, which some of the pilots attended, while most of the remainder played baseball and won with only one ringer, the YMCA man as pitcher. An escort was provided for some big formations of bombers, going out about midnight.

June 24 The heat wave is still with us but there are really no complaints as memories of the cold at Castletown last winter are still green. A sergeant-pilot reported to the Squadron but as he has had all his training on Spitfires there would appear to be a mistake somewhere, most probably in London where they usually originate.

June 25 An old boy of the Squadron, F/L T.B. Little, now with 402, had a narrow escape when his dinghy inflated in the cockpit so that he was out of control. He managed to pull out the pin on his Sutton harness and punctured the rubber just in time. Some spikes are now being installed in our Hurricanes in case of any future trouble of this kind.

June 27 The mess was crowded with visitors, male and female, in the evening for a dance. Our Lothario, F/O Blake Wallace, now known as "Playboy," deemed the occasion worthy of wearing his store teeth.

June 28 About seventy-four of the Squadron, including many of the original lot, got their orders to go back to Canada. They were practically all NCOs and it cannot be said they were in tears on leaving.

June 30 There is a report that F/O Weston may be transferred to drogue-towing on account of coming in to land, and guess what. Due to the wisecracks we have been enduring on the relative merits of the Spitfire and Hurricane, it can be pointed out here that they have at least one thing in common — wheels to land on.

July 1 Our second Dominion Day overseas. The Squadron was ordered to stand by for a circus, [but it was] cancelled during the early afternoon. P/O Hugh Godefroy, who has been monopolizing the telephone in the mess, had a call today that was not nearly as pleasant as usual. An irate father warned him off, but as the caller would not give his name, our hero does not know which one to lay off, so possibly he will be seen around our home in the evenings more frequently and keep his mind on his work.

July 3 A sweep over northern France was carried out. Enemy a/c, out of range, were seen and engaged by a Spitfire squadron. Our a/c [had] no action to report.

July 5 This business of being the only operational Squadron on the station with nobody to share the duties is becoming a trifle tiresome, with early morning readiness, dusk readiness, night fighter and the sweeps [over France] in between.
  With W/C McGregor leading, the Squadron made a tour of France as far as St. Omer, then, returning to the coast, watched [escorted] the bombers, which were Stirlings this time, return home. It was a pleasant outing, no Jerries being seen, no a/a fire, just nothing. F/L Morrison had a momentary tightening of the well-known strings when his

motor cut out with magneto trouble, but he managed to keep it going enough to get to Manston for repairs.

July 8   Court martials for anybody found with 100-octane fuel [in their cars] and also for low flying. They are taking samples out of gas tanks near Nottingham and unfortunately one airman was caught the other day. Pilots' cars will not be used so much from now on and it looks like bicycles.

July 9   The break-up of this Squadron goes on — in addition to the eight we have lost in the last month or so. [Headquarters] now insist that someone be detailed for instructor's duties at an OTU [operational training unit] so F/O Elliott will be leaving us in a few days. As it is anticipated that he will take Hamish [mongrel] with him, the chickens in the neighborhood will breathe freely again. Talking of chickens brings to mind that F/O E.L. Neal, president of the mess committee, is very busy trying to beat the government ration of one egg per person per week.

July 11   A dance in the evening resulted in the panel [truck] getting wrecked and the MT corporal having his arm broken. Possibly this has no connection with it being payday but it is curious and it is believed that dances are out for a while.

July 12   Nottingham on forty-eight-hours leave took its toll as F/Os Wallace and Connell got back, the former suffering from hallucinations and the latter from general lassitude and debility.

July 19   The Honorable C.G. Power, Canadian Minister of State for Air, and the Chief of Air Staff arrived. The pilots were introduced in turn and after a brief chat they left.

July 22   The day started off as usual with nothing to get excited about.

July 23 The Squadron took off at 1940 hours accompanied by 266 and 601 Squadrons for their jaunt over the French coast, acting as rear cover to our returning bombers. At long last F/O Neal got in a squirt at a couple of ME-109s. Sgt Northcott was hit and was forced to crash-land near Rolvenden, hitting a pole, and his a/c turned over. He is reported as suffering from shock but doing well.

July 24 After cruising around over the French coast, nothing happened to prevent the Squadron from returning to base intact.

July 29 The dusk patrol was also cancelled. Here endeth a dull day.

August 6 While awaiting further instructions [for a sweep over France] a game of the inevitable "red dog" developed and raged for some time. Some will be minus spare change for some time to come.

August 7 A sweep over northern France was carried out in company with Squadrons 257 and 19. The Wing's duty was rear cover for the bombers and their escort wings. Near St. Omer the Wing was attacked by ME-109s which dived down at high speed out of the sun. P/O T.K. Coupland was shot down and three of the Spitfires of 19 Squadron were lost. Owing to the enemy tactics no one of this Squadron was able to engage. Everyone will miss that lovable chap, quiet and unassuming "Coupy."

August 8 During one of five scrambles between 1430 and 1916 hours, F/O Neal was patrolling off the coast north of Skegness when he saw a bandit JU-88 skimming the cloud tops. With a tremendous burst of speed and enthusiasm he tore down on the JU-88 and hurled everything he had at it except his airscrew, causing the e/a's starboard engine to smoke. The e/a was last seen in a steep bank disappearing into cloud. Unfortunately the enemy's return fire hit an oil line and he was afterwards forced to crash-land near Horncastle in a wheat field, much to the chagrin of the farmer who did much worrying about his crop. F/O Neal returned to Coningsby and was picked up by F/O McColl in the Maggie [Magister plane]. He was full of apologies about his a/c.

August 10   This condition [night off duty] produced one of the greatest blitzes ever seen and heard in the [mess]. There was more beer thrown than consumed.

August 15   S/L Nesbitt left on a forty-eight-hour leave followed closely by F/L Blaiklock and F/O McColl, destination of all being London. Can London take it?

August 19   The CO returned from his visit with the Commander-in-Chief with the news that the Squadron was to be re-equipped with Spitfires very soon. It was also learned that S/L Nesbitt will be returning to Canada shortly after twelve months of operational duty with this Squadron which included the months of intense fighting during the summer last year. [A medical report on this date to RCAF Headquarters in Ottawa said Squadron health was good, with no cases of venereal disease.]

August 22   Cecil Beaton, photographer to the Queen, accompanied by the press liaison officer, 12 Group, came around to dispersal and took a number of snaps of the pilots in various groups and individual poses. P/O Al Harley and Sgt Thompson obliged with great enthusiasm to a request for a couple of dives past the photographer. Capt. Montgomery is still in hospital and is reported doing well, but talked several neighboring patients into a relapse.

August 23   W/C Woods [RAF] and Mrs. Woods gave a party in honor of our S/L Nesbitt and it turned out to be a pip. P/O Harley had been to Lincoln in the afternoon and visited a novelty shop, buying a lot of trick gadgets. Presently even your best friend could not be trusted and cigarettes, pipes or cigars were liable to explode at any moment. Trick spiders were found in beer glasses. S/L Nesbitt suggested that as our host had been so very nice to us, the least we could do was to show our usual appreciation, and the W/C was lifted bodily and deposited outside in the rain. The CO acted as bartender with an impromptu bar in the rear of the panel [truck] to make the return trip more memorable.

August 27 It was a gay old evening [the third farewell party for Nesbitt] and somebody got the idea that they would like a souvenir of one of the chief's buttons, which precipitated an avalanche, leaving him looking like a chorus girl after a losing night at strip poker.

September 6 The Right Honorable Mackenzie King, Prime Minister of Canada, visited the Squadron today, accompanied by a large entourage of press photographers and liaison officers. After being introduced to the officers and sergeant-pilots, he spoke briefly and climbed into a Hurricane cockpit, aided by F/L Bud Connell who shared in reflected glory and was photographed about a hundred times.

September 7 Three new Spitfires were received today — the first a/c of this type used by the Squadron.

September 10 The Squadron played soccer against 409 Squadron, but regardless of our undoubted superiority the score still stands at 9 to 0 against us.

September 14 There were four patrols and ground strafing of troops enjoyed in a practice invasion exercise. This last is a very popular form of work in these parts.

September 17 Col. [George] Drew [premier of Ontario] from good old Canada came around to dispersal for a visit and was shown around and introduced to the pilots by S/L Johnstone.

September 21 The Squadron was declared non-operational last night so that the conversion to Spits will be expedited. The Hurricanes will be laid away in mothballs and all available Spits will be worked overtime.

October 5 The Squadron is now almost completely equipped with the new Spitfire V-B.

October 7 The fog closed in solidly again in late afternoon and at about 7 p.m. two Oxfords which had been caught in the fog could be heard circling overhead with no possible chance of getting down. It was learned later that they all baled out safely though some suffered minor injuries when they landed.

October 9 S/L Johnstone returned from his leave and looked very fit. He said that this was the result of a lot of time spent in bed — resting.

October 11 It was learned that a former member of this Squadron, F/L Freddie Watson, crashed last night and was killed. He was flying a Defiant at 1,600 feet when his instruments went haywire. After telling his gunner to bale out, Freddie failed to do so himself and crashed with his a/c south of The Wash.

October 13 The CO, S/L Johnstone, left this afternoon for London to attend a conference in connection with our move [to Biggin Hill]. F/O Neal no doubt momentarily thought over his past sins when he was flying at 30,000 feet. An object left in his cockpit jammed his control column and he dove in a semi-inverted position to within a few feet of the ground. That isn't our idea of good clean fun.

October 16 The CO and F/L Connell returned from a London conference and brought back horror reports of PT parades at 6 a.m. and other pleasantries to be expected at our new station. P/O Wally Floody had an unfortunate experience when having the cannon on his a/c tested. An expert from the factory was attempting to discover the cause of a stoppage when suddenly five rounds were fired, killing the factory man who was at Wally's side.

BIGGIN HILL, ENGLAND

October 20   The Squadron moved to Biggin Hill today. All serviceable a/c were flown down and arrived during the afternoon. The ground personnel were taken by road convoy, leaving at 0720 hours, and arrived at approximately 1600 hours. Quarters were found to be comfortable and unloading the vehicles proceeded preparatory to starting normal operations next day.

October 21   A twelve-aircraft fighter sweep in company with 609 and 72 Squadrons was carried out over northern France. One section encountered a number of ME-109s. At 27,000 feet F/O Blake Wallace saw a dogfight below him and dove down to join in, followed by P/O Small and Sgts Thompson and Whitson. Blake saw a Spitfire being attacked by an ME-109 and finished the argument with a three-second burst of cannon. He was then attacked by another ME-109 who put one round in the ammunition box of one of his m/gs, which later caused a jam. Blake went after this fellow who had climbed away and was circling above. Blake climbed after him, got inside the e/a's circle and gave him the benefits of all his ammunition. The last seen of this chap, he was going down in a vertical dive with black smoke pouring from his a/c. However, Sgt Whitson who followed Blake down into the fight was not seen afterward and is still missing. A wild but extremely likeable chap is Whitty and we still have hopes of hearing from him.

October 25   F/O Wallace flew down to Bournemouth [RCAF arrival depot] to see his brothers who have come over recently and are both sergeant-pilots.

October 27 The day broke bright and clear for this time of the year. At 1120 we received word that a fighter sweep would be done over France. The Squadron took off at 1135 with 609 Squadron and after rendezvousing with 72 Squadron over Manston proceeded over the Channel toward France. S/L Johnstone was forced to return with oxygen trouble and Sgt Northcott returned with engine trouble. North of Poperinge P/O Al Harley noticed Spitfires on his port and starboard suddenly go down out of control. Immediately after, several ME-109s dove past him and he followed them down, getting two bursts at one which he saw pouring out black smoke before he broke away at 12,000 feet. He then found himself alone, so returned to base. It later turned out that the Wing had been jumped by about fifty e/a, mostly ME-109s and FW-190s. P/O Harley was credited with one ME-109 damaged and F/O Neal with one ME-109 probable and one damaged. F/O Wallace and P/O Small are sharing one e/a. S/P S.L. Thompson's a/c crashed near Deal. The pilot was heard to say he was baling out. His body was found near his a/c, parachute unopened. Four pilots are missing: F/O Wallace, P/O J.A. Small, P/O C.W. Floody and Sgt B.G. Hodgkinson. No report concerning them has been received. F/O Neal crash-landed near Rye but sustained no injuries. [His a/c had been damaged by enemy action.] S/P Whitney baled out and landed near Sandwich. He baled out at 600 feet but his 'chute did not open until he was within approximately 100 feet of the ground. He landed quite heavily but was uninjured.

All in all, the worst day the Squadron has ever experienced [or was ever to experience] and five familiar and popular faces missing from our entourage — we still have hopes of hearing from some of them, though. It was certainly a blue Monday for the Squadron.

October 28 More was learned of yesterday's operations when F/O Neal returned. He had been flying with Red section led by F/O Wallace with F/O Johnny Small and P/O Wally Floody. They were suddenly attacked by about fifteen ME-109s and P/O Floody was seen to go down. F/O Neal's a/c was hit by cannon fire and he turned sharply to port, got on the e/a's tail and fired a three-second burst with both cannon and machine-gun. There were two explosions behind the e/a cockpit and he pulled up sharply, flicked over into a spin and went down. F/O Neal was again attacked and fired a short burst and saw pieces fly off the fuselage and the e/a broke away. The remaining ME-109s turned and attacked him, hitting his fuselage, so he turned toward the English coast and was forced to crash-land near Rye. During the first part of his combat he saw two a/c go down burning, one of which was definitely an ME-109 and was undoubtedly shot down by F/O Wallace or P/O Small or both of them. Sgt Whitney was flying back from France at 20,000 feet, behind F/L Connell and Sgt Thompson, when he was attacked from out of the sun by e/a who hit his a/c with cannon fire. He turned sharply to port to evade but was again hit. He limped along to the English coast and was forced to bale out when his engine broke into flames. He got clear at 500 feet, his parachute opening at 100 feet. Sgt Thompson's a/c was apparently hit in the same attack and he baled out just inside the English coast. Unfortunately, when he left the a/c he must have hit his head on the tailplane and was stunned, because he made no attempt to pull the rip-cord and was killed. Damned rotten luck if ever there was! Words cannot describe one's feelings about this tough luck, but we know the Squadron has suffered a tremendous loss and we personally the finest friends one could wish for.

October 29 Four newcomers reported to the Squadron.

October 31 The funeral of Sgt Thompson was held at Brookwood Cemetery. Representatives from various RCAF units were present.

One of the most difficult (and unending) ground duties for a squadron commanding officer was to write to the next-of-kin of killed and missing fliers. Most of these casualty letters held to a fairly standard format and photographs of funerals were always included wherever possible, but most COs tried to add some personal touch that raised the letter above the harsh style of the dreaded defence department telegram which the family would have already received. Only a few such letters from 401 commanders have been preserved in the National Archives. S/L N.R. Johnstone, CO of 401, wrote to James Thompson of Davidson, Saskatchewan, after his son, Sgt Stanley L. Thompson, was killed on the disastrous October 27 sweep:

> Stanley's loss has been severely felt by this Squadron, both as a pilot and as a gentleman.
>
> Your son was buried Friday afternoon in the RCAF plot at Brookwood Cemetery near Woking, Surrey. The service was conducted by S/L W.E. Cockram, our Canadian padre, and full Military Honors were accorded. I am enclosing several photographs of the funeral service which I attended with several of his closest friends.

November 5 A group of American officers visited dispersal and was shown around by our F/Ls Morrison and Connell. This is a very common occurrence at this station and groups from various countries are coming and going continually.

November 6 News was received that Sgt Whitson, missing after operations October 21, is slightly wounded and is a prisoner of war.

November 7 There was a lecture on prisoners of war. It was an interesting talk by Capt. Bennett who is experienced in that sort of thing, having escaped from Germany during the last war, 1914-1918.

November 8 401 was jumped [over France] by a number of ME-109s, repeated attacks being made on our formation. After the Squadron's return it was learned that F/O Scruffy Weir and Sgt Gardner were missing. Sgt Gardner has not been with the Squadron for very long but had developed rapidly into a very real asset and was very well liked by all. F/O Weir had been an institution in the Squadron and one could not hope for a more likeable, fun-loving chap.

November 11 P/Os Gilbert, Blakeslee and Hutchinson departed in P/O Gilbert's "gas chariot" [for a night in town]. Alas! everything went wrong and most of the night was spent in pushing the "chariot" along the road in a heavy downpour.

November 12 The Squadron is losing our Jack Morrison who is now a Sir [Squadron Leader] and is going to 412 Squadron as commanding officer.

November 13 This was another day which started with a steady and heavy downpour. A low-flying mist also helped to make the weather completely u/s. Consequently the pilots' hut was the scene of a constantly changing financial status. A signal from Air Ministry states that P/O C.W. Floody and Sgt B.G. Hodgkinson are slightly wounded and prisoners of war. P/O J.A. Small was reported to have been killed.

Wally Floody might be a prisoner, but he wasn't idle. In civilian life he had worked for a Canadian gold-mining company and during all his years of captivity he took a leading part in all escape activities, devising many tunnelling techniques. He was not only an organizer, but a tunneller. He was twice buried under heavy falls of sand but was rescued by quick-thinking and fast-acting fellow diggers.

Floody was largely responsible for the construction of the tunnel through which seventy-six officers escaped from Stalag Luft III in March 1944. (Most were recaptured and shot.) His courage and devotion to the cause of escape helped build and maintain morale among the prisoners and Floody is still spoken of today with respect and admiration.

Floody died in Toronto in 1989. His death was ignored by nearly all Canadian newspapers but it was the lead obituary in *The Times* of London, September 27.

November 15 F/L Connell checked up as a matter of interest on the turnover of pilots since Prestwick days and it is exactly fifty in one year.

November 18 [Over the French coast] F/O Hank Sprague opened her up wide and tackled the leading ME-109 with cannon and it poured out smoke, turned over and went straight down, giving Hank a probable. P/O Blakeslee fired a short burst and broke away immediately. He did not notice the result but P/O Gilbert coming from behind noticed pieces flying from the a/c. Gilbert then fired a five-second burst at another ME and pieces flew off, including one which appeared to be the starboard aileron. It then turned over on its back and spiralled down into cloud. That gave Gilbert a probable and Blakeslee a damaged. F/L Neal, after crossing the French coast, screamed down on a number of ME-109s, fired a five- or six-second burst with cannon and was followed by Sgt Don Morrison, who was on his first trip over France, who fired another burst. This ME flew straight for a few seconds, then a thin brownish smoke poured out, then gradually thickened till it enveloped the fuselage and it turned over and went down, disappearing into cloud below. F/L Neal and Sgt Morrison shared a probable. All our pilots returned safely.

November 20 There was a mess dinner and Commander Stephen King Hall was the guest speaker. He spoke very casually of the possible progress of the war in 1943.

November 21 The only flying was a three-hour convoy patrol. Visibility closed in around 1500 hours and Sgt C.R. Golden crash-landed at Maidstone, Kent. He was admitted to hospital suffering from a fractured thigh, lacerations to knees and face, and shock. He was posted to non-effective.

November 22 The Squadron in company with 72 Squadron carried out a sweep over northern France. Considerable numbers of e/a were encountered with resultant score for our Squadron of two ME-109s and three FW-190s destroyed, one FW-190 probably destroyed, and one FW-190 and three ME-109s damaged.

When at 17,000 feet, the Wingco noticed about fifteen e/a coming south at about 6,000 feet toward Boulogne and he detailed our Yellow and Blue Sections to go down and attack while he remained above with Red Section as top cover. Yellow Section, composed of F/L Neal, P/O Ormston, P/O Blakeslee and Sgt Morrison went screaming down into the flock of Jerries and when the smoke had cleared away Ormston had destroyed an ME-109. Blakeslee had also destroyed an ME-109 and damaged another. Sgt Morrison had destroyed an FW-190 and also damaged one. F/L Neal was attacked by three FW-190s [en route home] but Sgt Morrison jumped the rearmost and sent him crashing into the Channel. Sgt Omer J.A. Levesque had a running fight with several FW-190s, destroying one and probably destroying another. S/L Johnstone and Sgt Northcott damaged an ME-109 each. F/O H.A. Sprague is missing.

November 23 Official photographers visited the Squadron to interview pilots about the operations carried out the day before.

November 24 It has been learned that F/O Scruffy Weir is a prisoner of war but is said to be seriously wounded.

November 27 A sortie to London by most of the officers took place, all crowding into one railway compartment, F/L Neal resorting to the luggage rack as seating accommodation. There were reports of a raid on the Estuary but it may have been only our boys making merry at the Park Lane, etc.

November 30 It was learned early this morning that Sgt Gardner, who was missing after an offensive operation over France, is dead.

December 2 F/L Neal and Sgt Whitney travelled by train to Halton to visit Sgt Golden, in hospital there since his crash. "Goldie" is improving, though he will be trussed up for some time to come.

December 4 A group of pilots went to Perley in the evening where an excellent ice-skating rink exists, and it is suggested as a good place to spend odd evenings.

December 8 At 1355 the Squadron again took off on a Channel sweep to protect rescue launches trying to locate the pilots who had come down in the Channel during morning operations. Three or four ME-109s dived to attack Blue Section and were in turn attacked by our other sections, and a series of dogfights took place. Sgt D.R. Morrison destroyed one ME-109, the e/a crashing in the Channel, and he also damaged another. P/O Don Blakeslee and Sgts G.B. Whitney and W.D. Hagyard damaged one each. There were no casualties in our Squadron.

December 10 Notification was received through the International Red Cross from Berlin that F/O H.A. Sprague, missing on November 22, is now a prisoner of war.

December 12 In answer to a call for volunteers to go to the Middle East, almost all the pilots put in their names. P/O Don Gilbert and Sgt Mathews got the call and if they survive various inoculations will go east. Our new pilot officer, Jeff Northcott, appeared in the mess in his new uniform, drinks were served up and everything got into a rather hilarious state. A snooker game got under way and P/O Gilbert stretched out on the table to pot an easy shot but fell asleep instead.

December 21 [The Squadron returned from Manston where it had been fog-bound for four days.] The boys looked for all the world like a submarine crew after a long voyage in mid-ocean with long beards. In the meantime, their shaving kits had been sent down to Manston and should be back here again just after they have taken off again for Manston.

December 22 Much amusement was had at the expense of the pilots whose thrilling exploits in a recent combat were vividly described in Canadian newspapers and read to them in the dispersal hut.

December 25 Christmas Day, the second one overseas for this Squadron. Flying for the day consisted of local and formation practice. In the airmen's mess at noon all personnel sat down to Christmas dinner. They were waited on by officers, which seemed to appeal to them greatly. F/L Neal was requested by the WAAFs as their waiter and did a bang-up job on this assignment. The dinner was good considering conditions of food rationing.

1942

THE ALLIES SLOGGED AWAY on all fronts trying to hold their own or, where possible here and there, to turn the enemy tide. S/L Leonard Birchall of the RCAF's 413 Squadron spotted a Japanese fleet in the Indian Ocean and managed to radio a warning that saved Ceylon before he and his crew were shot down. Another RCAF squadron, 417, joined the Desert Air Force in Egypt. Still another, 111, went to the Aleutians for operations against the Japanese occupying Kiska. The Royal Canadian Navy was heavily engaged in the grinding war of the North Atlantic convoys. RCAF bombers took part in the first 1,000-plane raid on Germany. The Canadian Army suffered grievous losses in its raid on the French coast at Dieppe. No. 1 Squadron remained in the southeast of England, patrolling against enemy raids while raiding the enemy in occupied France.

BIGGIN HILL, ENGLAND

January 1 The Squadron has acquired a new call sign which has not been hailed with much enthusiasm, it being no other than "Dearie." [The call sign for the huge airfield at Manston was "Manlove."]

Another year has rolled around and the war goes merrily on with various speakers on the radio predicting more years of war to follow, which means that some of us will return to Canada sporting long white beards and black canes.

January 5 The Canadian concert group named the Tin Hats gave a concert in the station cinema hall, playing to a sellout crowd who thoroughly enjoyed it.

January 8 A soccer game was contemplated seriously by some of the more energetic souls, but after a hearty lunch this was called off in favor of a game of snooker. [In the evening] the station party got going in earnest. Before it was over most of the elite, including the Group Captain, were de-bagged and their trousers used to decorate the piano. Two culprits backed themselves into the bar but were foiled by W/C Sailor Malan [South African ace] who made a surprise attack sans trousers through the rear window to dislodge them.

January 13 One could almost imagine he was in Canada this morning as there was a snowfall during the night and, strange to relate, it was still on the ground this morning.

January 14 The time is taken up these days in much the same manner: when the weather permits, the maximum practice flying is done, this being mostly cinegun, air firing, formation and dog-fighting practice. Readiness flying is practically all convoy patrol work, this being often done in very unfavorable weather conditions.

January 15 A group of pilots went over to the Perley ice rink while a few played bridge as their contribution to the sports program.

January 26 S/L Norm Johnstone is leaving the Squadron and is to be replaced by S/L A.G. Douglas, RAF, a former CO of 403 Squadron who has taken part in more than forty wing sweeps over France and has several e/a to his credit. [Douglas was 401's only non-Canadian commanding officer.]

January 28 The Wingco [W/C Stanford-Tuck, RAF] went inland south of Berck [with P/O Al Harley] and executed a wide circle at ground level, returning to a point just northwest of Boulogne where a gun post opened up on them. The Wingco turned to the right and P/O Harley turned to the left, hitting a treetop. The Wingco's a/c was emitting white smoke when last seen and he has not returned from this operation. Harley had a considerable portion of the French forests in his oil cooler when he returned.

January 31   A large group descended on the country club at Bromley. It included most of the chaps who will constitute our hockey team at Perley against 400 Squadron and it does not augur well for their condition.

February 1   A heavy snowfall was under way as the hockey team [Biggin Bears] met at dispersal. A start was made at 0845 in a large lorry. [400 Squadron was stranded at East Croydon station and the game got under way at 1145 after transport was sent to pick them up.] The game became very fast and heavy body checks were handed out freely. The game ended with the score 3 to 2 in favor of 400 Squadron. The 401 boys seemed tired, which may or may not have been caused by the country club callisthenics the previous evening. The trip home through the snow was long and cold.

February 5   A kit inspection has been carried out in the past two days which was most revealing.

February 6   Two films were loaned from a Bromley company. One brought to mind the remarkable about-face of feeling toward the Russians. Among other things [the old film] described the Russians as bullies.

February 9   There was SFA doing during the day as old man weather had the index digit in.

February 11   Six Spits were ordered off to beat up some ships just off Dunkirk. Three fairly large merchant ships were banged at. F/S W.D. (Will) Hagyard did not return. He called up saying he had been badly hit and did not think he could make it. The other boys, try as they did, could not locate him. He will certainly be missed as he was tops with all the gang.

February 12 Today was one of the most spectacular days since Dunkirk [1940 evacuation]. The battleships *Scharnhorst* and *Gneisenau* and the cruiser *Prinz Eugen* escorted by twenty to thirty other naval units steamed up through the Channel. Practically all available a/c in the Group were rushing out to get a wallop. The Jerry ships were covered by swarms of ME-109s and FW-190s. Our boys took off shortly after noon and joined action about thirty minutes later. P/O I.C. (Ormie) Ormston nailed a 109, then joined Harley and Sgt Don Morrison and the three of them bagged another. P/O Levesque, followed by Sgt MacDonald, engaged a swarm of Jerries and chased them in and out of France in a mad whirl. Sgt MacDonald got a damaged and Levesque did not return. He will certainly be missed — we feel certain that he brought at least one down with him.

February 24 Sgt Pope, who was flying LAC O'Briend, an armorer [in the Magister], ran afoul of a down draught on his approach and made a neat three-point landing in the top of a tree. The tree settled down to the earth gently, depositing the Maggie at an ungainly angle in a hedge. Both Sgt Pope and his passenger were unhurt. The Maggie, however, was a rather pathetic sight to behold.

February 25 Word was received that P/O Levesque, missing after the *Scharnhorst* do, is a prisoner of war and slightly wounded. A most regrettable accident occurred when Cpl Turgeon was killed near the south gate, being crushed under a heavy vehicle and dying four hours later.

February 26 There was an exhibition of tanks on the drill square during which several of the pilots drove and rode in some of the various types, including the largest British tank, the Churchill.

February 28 On the return trip [from Ostend, covering Blenheim bombers] at about mid-Channel, the Squadron was attacked by ME-109s and FW-190s. Sgt Clarke reported himself as hit but was not seen by other pilots of the Squadron. P/O Ormston was attacked from above and astern by an FW-190 which passed over Sgt Morrison. Morrison followed and as the e/a broke away, banking sharply to starboard, fired a two-second burst from 250 to 300 yards. He saw his shells bursting inside the e/a's cockpit and on top of the engine. The e/a slowly turned over on its back and went straight down, emitting black smoke. Sgt Clarke did not return and is missing.

March 7 P/O Hugh Godefroy was married today at Tunbridge Wells. The bride was Asst. Section Officer Constance Jessie Helm, a WAAF officer of this station [Biggin Hill].

March 9 While executing a practice roll over Fairfield, Kent, Sgt A.D. Blakey remained in an inverted position. A large part of his port wing fell off and the a/c went straight down from 5,000 feet, crashed and burst into flames. The pilot remained in the a/c and was killed.

March 10 F/L Bill Napier made a forced landing at Gatwick after a sweep over the Channel. It was rather a close call for Bill as another Spit swept over his a/c in mid-Channel and knocked off about six inches of his prop.

March 12 Asst. Section Officer Helm or Mrs. Hugh Godefroy visited the dispersal hut, causing P/O Don Blakeslee no end of embarrassment when she was introduced by exclaiming, "So you are the sheik of 401."

March 13 About five miles west of St. Omer, F/S Whitham followed an FW-190 down at 400 mph, firing all his ammo. At about 1,500 feet the e/a turned on its back and continued its near-vertical dive. Whitham blacked out completely in pulling out, levelling out at 500 feet. The e/a was claimed as destroyed as it could not have pulled out of its dive at the speed and altitude when last seen. S/L Douglas fired a one-second burst from 100 yards and [another] FW-190 flew south with a heavy trail of blackish smoke coming from underneath the engine. This was definitely not ha-ha [artificial smoke trail] and the e/a was claimed as probably destroyed. S/L Douglas's a/c was badly damaged and after nursing it to the English coast he baled out, landing in a field near the village of Woodchurch, Kent. He was uninjured. His method of baling out was first jettisoning the hood, then pushing the stick forward which threw him clear.

March 17 This being St. Patrick's Day, the boys celebrated by painting a very beautiful shamrock on S/P Duff's unwilling tummy.

March 18 A dinner was given in honor of 401, the outgoing Squadron [to Gravesend]. Beverley Baxter, MP, gave a humorous but very interesting talk.

GRAVESEND, ENGLAND

March 19 Officers are quartered at Cobham Hall, about three miles from the station, while airmen are billeted in Nissen huts about two miles from the station. Sergeant-pilots are billeted in a former tea house called Pol Perro which is adjacent to the station.

Airmen's mail was regularly intercepted and read, ostensibly to check security and morale. RCAF Headquarters in London sent to 401's CO, S/L Douglas, this letter written by LAC D. Wright to a relative in Winnipeg: "Here [Gravesend] we have to stand guard on the gates and they have plenty of Englishmen around here doing nothing that could do it but that English CO [Douglas] we have won't stick up for us." The Archives file containing this letter does not record whether Wright was reprimanded. Another 401 airman, Nelson Bowenfaut, was reported by RCAF Headquarters to the CO because in a letter home he had mentioned winning £4 in a crap game. Still another was snitched on because he had reported to his family that he had been successful in scrounging a pailful of coal. This gives another indication of how Headquarters prosecuted the war.

March 20 Lt.-Gen. B.L. Montgomery, GOC, Southeast Command, visited the Squadron dispersal points.

March 24 F/S Jack Ferguson was forced to crash-land near Bobbing, Kent. His a/c turned over, pinning him inside. His engine was on fire but prompt work by [British soldiers] who brought a fire extinguisher with them saved the day for the pilot.

April 10 The Squadron proceeded to Biggin Hill at 1540 hours to be briefed for an operation over France. While being briefed with the Wing, another operation requiring one squadron only, to escort Hurri-bombers, came through and this Squadron was selected for the job. After awaiting details of, and the order to, take off for about an hour, the operation was cancelled.

April 19 The scheduled operation over France was cancelled and the Squadron went to lunch.

April 28 About five miles south of Dunkirk combats took place with FW-190s as a result of which P/O D.J.M. Blakeslee claimed two FW-190s probably destroyed. Blakeslee fired a short burst at one a/c from 800 yards, then engaged another FW-190 in a head-on attack, seeing his ammo explode in the e/a's engine. Immediately after the latter had gone down spinning with smoke pouring from it, a third FW-190 was engaged in the same manner with the same effect but it went down in a slower spin and was emitting a smaller trail of smoke. P/O Jack Ferguson is missing and P/O G.B. Whitney's a/c was seen falling onto Manchester Road, Whitfield, Kent. He had not baled out and was killed when the a/c crashed and exploded, his body being thrown clear.

May 1 Our Yellow Section [four planes] circled twice below cloud in an area approximately fifteen miles west of Le Havre and was jumped by ME-109s, two first followed by ten or eleven more. F/L E.L. Neal saw P/O Patton being hit and he went down from 7,000 feet, his a/c hitting the water. Neal was attacked by two ME-109s, one of whose bullets struck the glycol radiator and two cannon shells striking the starboard wing from underneath. Smoke started to fill the cockpit so he gave a "m'aidez" [Mayday], removed his helmet, wound the trimming tabs fully forward, then baled out, striking his head and knee on the aerial post. He was very slightly injured. The position was approximately twenty-five or thirty miles south of Portsmouth. After being in the sea for two hours he was picked up by a rescue boat and brought to Portsmouth. It is of interest that a fix of his position was received from the German RDF [radio direction finding] through [British intelligence].

May 9 Three bandits were reported over St. Omer but [we] saw nothing and came out at Le Touquet. The pilots of 401 saw a splash in the water just south of Dungeness which later proved to have been made when P/O Waters of 72 Squadron went into the sea from an unknown cause and is missing.

May 14 It was learned in the evening that S/L A.G. Douglas, F/L E.L. Neal and F/L I.C. Ormston of this Squadron had been awarded the DFC.

May 16 S/L Douglas called the pilots and ground crews for a short talk in which he thanked the pilots and ground personnel for their good work which had culminated in the recognition for the Squadron in the persons of the CO and flight commanders.

May 17 The CO, flight commanders and other pilots put four Spitfire VIs through their paces. These a/c had been flown to the aerodrome from Wittering for the purpose of obtaining the opinion of the pilots as to its merits. On the whole, the pilots were not impressed.

May 24 Red 3, F/S Morrison, saw several FW-190s below and attacked one from astern quarter to dead astern, closing to 100 yards with four- or five-second burst of cannon and m/g. He saw cannon strikes on the starboard wing followed by a flash which appeared to be an exploding magazine. He followed the e/a down to 10,000 feet, then broke away when he saw several more e/a above him. He climbed to 20,000 feet in mid-Channel, then turned back toward France in the direction of Calais when he saw a Spitfire diving toward home from the Gris Nez area followed by an FW-190 about 800 yards behind at approximately 15,000 feet. Morrison made a steep diving turn to the right and attacked at 10,000 feet from rear quarter to astern with an eight- or nine-second burst, firing until his tracer ammo was gone. The e/a did a slight left-hand turn and dense white smoke poured from both wing roots when at approximately 8,000 feet he broke away and left the e/a still going down in a steep dive with the white smoke still pouring out. In both combats the e/a took no evasive action whatsoever. This led Morrison to believe that the pilot had either been badly hit or killed. Both a/c were claimed as damaged.

May 29 Blue 3 (F/L Ormston) and 4 (Sgt E.L. Gimbel) saw a Spitfire going northeast with a thin stream of white smoke coming from it and, with Red 3, accompanied it out to sea where the pilot was seen to bale out and the a/c dive into the sea. The pilot came down on the sea about twelve to sixteen miles northeast of Dunkirk, whereupon F/L Ormston and Red 3 gave several maydays from 3,000 feet. These were not satisfactory so the pilots climbed and gave more fixes, eventually reaching a height of 9,000 feet. At that level they were attacked by two FW-190s but maintained their orbiting, dodging the e/a which came in on repeated attacks. All a/c returned safely.

Our [air sea rescue patrol] continued to a point about eight miles offshore from Niewport, then west to a point off Dunkirk where the Spitfire pilot of 72 Squadron was last seen in the sea. This point was searched before proceeding offshore to Calais, then returned to base. At 1710 hours six a/c took off on air sea rescue patrol. A square from Calais to Ostend and twenty miles from the French coast was patrolled for one hour and ten minutes. There was nothing to report.

June 1 At 0600 hours two a/c took off with instructions to patrol the Hastings-Dover coastline. While on this patrol they were vectored onto two bandits plotted from the Calais area and approached the e/a which were silhouetted in the sun off Dover. Both were shot down by our pilots.

The Spitfire pilots were never identified. The 401 log for October 11, 1942, says: "These a/c proved to be two friendly Typhoons which were reported as enemy aircraft by ops. An investigation was held by Air Ministry and our two pilots were exonerated from all blame. This correction is made in accordance with RCAF HQ letter of September 1, 1942, S 22-1-401 (A.1)."

June 2 Yellow Section attacked a train standing at a station about twelve miles northeast of Le Tréport and then proceeded west where P/O Tucker exchanged "greetings" with a man on a bicycle on the road. The Section then attacked a wireless station just north of Ault.

June 3 A twin-engined, low-wing monoplane was seen about eight miles northeast of Le Tréport travelling toward Dieppe at about 100 to 120 mph. Red 1 (F/L Neal) pulled up in a right-hand turn at 500 feet and from astern fired a 1¼-second burst. This fire struck the starboard engine and wing root. Red 2 (F/S Cosburn) also opened fire with a three-second burst, closing to fifty yards. The e/a was seen to burst into flames and crash twenty or thirty seconds later. As the Squadron recrossed the French coast just north of Ault, Yellow 1 and 2 shot up a barracks building adjacent to a wireless station while Yellow 3 shot up a thirty-foot tower. [A letter from the intelligence section, 11 Group, dated August 3, 1942, said the plane shot down by Neal and Cosburn was an ME-108 carrying Oberstleutnant Hahn, the pilot, and a German staff officer and a wireless operator. All three were killed. Hahn was a German war ace.] S/L K.L.B. Hodson has taken over command from S/L Douglas.

June 5 Our a/c dived on ten to fifteen FW-190s right over Abbeville town and a general dogfight took place. F/S Morrison fired a ½-second burst at one FW-190 from astern and saw cannon strikes on the starboard side of the fuselage, followed by a puff of white smoke. He stopped firing as W/C Rankin crossed in front of him, firing at the same e/a. As the e/a started down there was an explosion and it spiralled before it hit the ground. During the combat P/O Smither was heard to say on the R/T that he was going down, and did not return.

June 15 All pilots, ground crew, and others scheduled to move to Eastchurch were all set with equipment packed, etc., when the move was cancelled at 1700 hours.

June 20 F/Ss Morrison and Murray were appointed to the rank of pilot officer. P/O Morrison was awarded the DFM.

July 13 The Squadron lost F/L Tyre and F/S Duff due to a collision over the Somme estuary. One a/c fell in the sea about 300 yards from shore and the other about a quarter mile inland. They were followed down by F/L Whitham and neither was seen to get out of his machine. The weather was fine over France.

July 21 [After a patrol over Dunkirk:] No e/a, no flak, no incidents, no casualties.

July 26 P/O Tucker failed to return. He was last seen by Red 3 when climbing up through cloud in mid-Channel. Permission was granted for six a/c to look for him in the sea, but there was no success.

July 31 Ground crew moved from Gravesend to Biggin Hill by transport.

BIGGIN HILL, ENGLAND

August 6 As appreciation to ground crew who serviced eighteen Spitfire IXs in ten days, pilots entertained personnel in the airmen's mess with beer and eats. Very good party. Everyone attended.

August 7 Letter received from Sgt Duff's father requesting any further news as to what happened to his son.

LYMPNE, ENGLAND

August 14 Ground crew arrived Lympne at 1230 hours and a/c at 1325. Officers' mess in Sir Philip Sassoon's home, grounds quite beautiful, terraced on slope toward flat coastline, swimming pool in front, house finished in Egyptian style, marble pillars and walls, sunken bathtubs in some bathrooms, marble in others, with chain toilets, very weird arrangement of winding narrow stairs connecting floors. Inner sun court, Turkish harem style, fountain in centre, pictures and most furniture and light fixtures removed. Many well-kept terraced hedges down slope of hill, initials P.S. on all the concrete balustrades. Summing it all up, anyone would know that a woman had little to do with the interior decorating or architecture. No. 133 Squadron, being here before and knowing the layout, got all the best rooms.

August 15 "A" flight scrambled to 5,000 feet over base to intercept raiders. Four bombs dropped on Folkestone from a considerable height. We did not contact e/a. [Ten pilots] paid the Odeon and Majestic a visit in Folkestone. Westhaver and MacKay got left in the dark and returned by devious routes in the morning.

August 17 [The Squadron escorted twelve B-17 American bombers to the marshalling yards at Rouen. Twelve pilots were involved in combat with FW-190s. F/L Whitham destroyed one and other pilots had five probables and one damaged.] P/O Ferguson is missing. No one saw him go down. Fergie is the oldest timer in the Squadron, having done over seventy sweeps. We all hope he is a prisoner of war.

F/S W.E. Rowthorn was evidently shot through the port aileron. He returned to base and banked left at 400 feet to come in for a landing. His a/c went into a spin, turning twice. He managed to level off just before hitting the ground in a field adjoining the north side of the aerodrome, but the port wing hit and the a/c was strewn many yards and caught fire. F/S Rowthorn was thrown out with his seat and was dragged away from the burning wreckage by a farmer and a constable who were fortunately near the scene. He was conscious when picked up and had sustained wounds of the forehead and multiple injuries to legs, hands and face. Condition serious. Before taking off on the do, F/S Reesor and Rowthorn tossed to see who would go. Rowthorn won and said, "I keep the penny for luck." We hope his luck holds and he pulls through. He is a spunky chap, full of fight.

Six weeks after P/O J.K. (Jack) Ferguson went missing, the Squadron received this letter from Irene Heller, a friend:

> He had a wee dog that he was very fond of and I have been wondering if he is well taken care of.
> I also sent a couple of parcels and some cigarettes two weeks ago and I wonder if you would be so kind

as to see that they are distributed among his fellow officers.

S/L Keith Hodson, the commanding officer, wrote back:

> Regarding his dog "Whisky," he continued to receive fond attention from several new masters. However, in a fight with a much larger dog on this station he became a "casualty" and had to be put away by the medical officer. He was buried beside the pilots' shack at the dispersal point on the aerodrome.

August 18 G/C Halling-Potts and W/C Thomas briefed all pilots of 133 and 401 Squadrons for a big commando raid by Canadians to "Jubilee" [Dieppe], giving maps and detailed instructions. Utmost secrecy to be maintained; everybody all keyed up and raring to go.

August 19 [The Squadron flew cover for twenty-four American B-17 Fortress bombers to Abbeville airfield in support of the Dieppe raid.] Intense heavy flak over target, bursting close to bombers. Very accurate bombing results were observed. All bombers returned safely.

S/L Hodson took the Squadron south toward Dieppe. He identified four twin-engine bombers as DO-217s and closed to fifty yards dead astern on the nearest Dornier and gave a four-second burst of cannon and machine-gun, saw cannon shell explode with flash in the tail assembly and many strikes along the fuselage. Claimed as damaged. F/S Zobell picked another DO-217 and, coming in from above and behind, started firing at 300 yards and observed strikes on the fuselage and wings. Claimed as damaged. Zobell had to break off the attack as he was fired on by an unknown aircraft and was hit through rudder, wings, perspex and reflector sight, receiving an eye injury. He brought his aircraft back to base. [F/S Cosburn claimed two Dorniers damaged and P/O Morrison was seen to shoot down an FW-190 in flames before he baled out safely.] Pilots returning from Dieppe reported the town was covered by smoke.

[The Squadron then put up a patrol over Dieppe at 23,000 feet.] Ground troops had withdrawn when we arrived over Dieppe and the convoy [assault force] had travelled some forty miles from the French coast. F/L Whitham reports: Five miles off the coast at Dieppe we were at 15,000 feet. S/P Morton Buckley failed to climb steeply enough and I saw two FW-190s attack him. I called him to break, he did a gentle weave and the FWs overshot him. Two more FW-190s attacked him and I warned him to break again. He did not take violent enough evasive action. I dove on the rear FW-190 attacking Buckley but the e/a had fired on him. He went down and crashed in the sea without baling out. We were then at 4,000 feet. I went into a steep right turn using full top rudder and throttle and the two FW-190s turned as tightly as I did and then they broke and I pounced on the tail of one FW-190 and opened fire from fifty yards, giving the e/a a seven-second burst, saw strikes all down the port side and wings and into the engine, also cannon flashes, pieces came off the fuselage and the engine poured black smoke. E/A went into a shallow dive toward the sea, two miles offshore. This e/a is claimed as probably destroyed.

F/S Reesor reports: S/P L. Armstrong got hit and went into a spin, baled out and got into his dinghy. I came down low and circled S/P Armstrong. He appeared to be uninjured as he waved.

[In the third action that day, the Squadron protected the returning convoy as it approached the English coast. No e/a were encountered.]

BIGGIN HILL, ENGLAND

August 20 [The Squadron moved back to Biggin Hill.] F/S Rowthorn died at 1430 hours yesterday. He put up a game fight but was too badly hurt to pull through. Air Ministry reports the following casualties from yesterday's show over Dieppe: enemy fighters, forty-eight destroyed, twenty-nine probably destroyed, eighty damaged; enemy bombers, forty-three destroyed, nine probably destroyed, sixty damaged. Our casualties: sixty-eight pilots and ninety-eight aircraft. [After the war, German documents showed that German losses totalled forty-eight destroyed and twenty-four damaged. The Canadian 2nd Division suffered 3,369 casualties in the disastrous raid on Dieppe, 907 of these killed. An alibi for it was concocted after the Normandy landings in 1944: Dieppe had provided valuable lessons that made Normandy a success.]

P/O Don Morrison reported back none the worse for his dip in the Channel and [says:] I did not have time to pay attention to what was going on below, but at a glance could see that there was activity on land, on water and in the air. I saw a single FW-190 just ahead and about 1,500 feet below me. I did a slipping barrel roll, losing height, and levelled out about 150 yards behind and slightly to the starboard and above the e/a. I opened fire with a two-second burst closing to twenty-five yards. I saw strikes all along the starboard side of the fuselage and several pieces which seemed about a foot long flew off from around the cowling. Just as both the e/a and myself ran into cloud, he exploded with a terrific flash of flame and black smoke. My windshield and hood were covered with oil and there was a terrific clatter as pieces of debris struck my a/c. I was quite unaware that my own a/c had been damaged. Suddenly my engine started to cough and the a/c shuddered violently. I realized I was going to have to bale out so I started to climb. My engine cut completely but I had managed to reach 2,000 feet. I took off my helmet, undid my straps and opened the hood. I crouched on the seat and then shoved the stick forward. My parachute became caught somehow and I figured I was about 200 to 250 feet above the water when I got clear. The a/c plunged into the water below me as my parachute opened. I pressed the quick release just as I hit the water. I inflated my dinghy without any trouble and climbed into it. Two a/c kept circling while the third (F/L Whitham) went for a rescue boat, which was not far away. I put up my flag, which aided the rescue boat to come straight to me. The a/c

of my own Squadron being short of petrol left me but another squadron circled me until I was picked up. I had been
in the water for only about fifteen minutes. The captain of
the HSL 177 [rescue boat] estimated my position as seventeen miles off Dieppe. I was picked up about 1110 hours
and immediately got into dry clothes. Unfortunately, I was
told that I would have to stay on the boat until it returned
to port at night, so I would miss the rest of the day's fun.
During the afternoon we went on several other crash calls
without success, often operating within sight of the French
coast. We saw the attack by bombers on the convoy beaten
off by heavy ack-ack fire. We saw the explosion and pall of
smoke caused by two Spitfires colliding head on. We saw
gunfire from the shore and from the boat and a/c laying
smoke screens. Later on in the afternoon two FW-190s
passed over us at about 5,000 feet. Shortly afterward, I saw
them attack and set on fire another air sea rescue boat (HSL
122). Knowing that we could not do much with our own
light armament, we raced back toward England to get the
help of a Navy boat (ML 513) which we had previously noticed. As we went back to the burning launch we saw another rescue boat (HSL 123) trying to give aid to the first
one. Suddenly four more FW-190s attacked, setting the second launch on fire. Two Spitfires appeared in answer to our
calls for help and we indicated the trouble ahead and they
set out. No sooner had they left us when six more FW-190s
dived down to attack us. We escaped serious damage but
our radio was put out of action. The trifling fire put up by
our own inadequate Lewis guns didn't bother the e/a in the
least, but the fire from the 20mm Oerlikon gun on the Navy
boat evidently struck them. I believe they ran out of ammunition, and they left us. We picked up the survivors of the
two burning launches, all in the water. The two rescue
boats were burning furiously and the ammunition aboard
was exploding. Spitfires arrived (91 Squadron) and circled
around us. We picked up fourteen survivors and the Navy
boat picked up four, I believe. There should have been
twenty-two. The e/a had also attacked the men as they

were in the water. Most of the men picked up were very badly wounded, so we returned to port at full throttle. One of the Spitfires escorted us to within six miles of Beachy Head, the other staying with the slower Navy boat. On the way home we also saw the convoy attacked. We raced into Newhaven where there was an ambulance waiting for us. We unloaded the wounded men and then went ashore ourselves.

I have been in a few tight spots myself, but I never felt so helpless as I did when we were being attacked by those FW-190s. It is a crime that such brave men as the crews of these rescue launches should be lost because of lack of armament and fighter protection.

August 22 Squadron released off station. The pilots and ground crew went to the country club. We had a good time, lots of girls and a good band. 307 Squadron (American) gave us their transport to come home — they walked; that is what we call hospitality. Hugh Merrit and Ted Wood running true to form wanted to sock somebody before we took off, but everyone got home without injury.

August 26 P/O Morrison was congratulated by G/C Halling-Potts, station commander, for his brilliant and heroic work on August 19, [noting that Morrison's written report] does not state he jumped overboard and saved a badly wounded ASR chap in the Channel.

P/O Ibby Ibbotson was approached by a ground crew to put a sweetheart's name on his kite. Ibby said, "No, it would flop over on its back and I could never fly straight and level."

August 28 [The Squadron was escorting twelve American Fortress bombers attacking an aircraft factory when it ran into more than forty FW-190s over Amiens.] F/S G.B. Murray, Blue 1, saw an FW-190 opening fire on Blue 4 (P/O Westhaver). Blue 1 did a steep climbing turn to starboard, telling Section to break. A half-roll brought Blue 1 onto the tail of the e/a firing on Blue 4, giving a one-second burst from a range of fifty yards from ten degrees above and behind. Strikes and flashes were observed along the fuselage at the side of the cockpit and on both wings. The e/a flipped over on its back twice, then spun down vertically, emitting a thin trail of black smoke.

P/O Ibbotson saw an FW-190 at four o'clock and broke to port, closing to 150 yards, and opened fire on the e/a using eighty-degree deflection and observed strikes all along the cockpit. The e/a flicked on its back, Ibbotson gave another burst and saw strikes in the belly. The e/a went into a spin to about 7,000 feet, then went down in a dive with every appearance that the pilot had been killed.

F/L Whitham was last seen in combat over Amiens. He failed to return and is listed as missing.

August 30 [On the missing Whitham being awarded the DFC:] We hope Jimmie will show up some day to wear his well-earned gong.

F/L James Whitham and S/P Morton Buckley had flown together in the Dieppe operation and Whitham had seen Buckley shot down. Mrs. M.M. Buckley of Fonthill, Ontario, the pilot's mother, wrote to the Squadron: "We wondered if F/L Whitham might know more which he wished to spare us." S/L Hodson replied December 26, 1942:

> Unfortunately F/L Whitham has since been killed and as the boys were flying by themselves there is no one left who could give positive information.
>
> Although it is very hard to say so, it would seem to be too much to hope now that your son would still be alive.

Not many letters of this type were that honest.

September 2 [Two 401 Spitfires were scrambled to intercept two FW-190s over the English coast.] P/O Morrison opened fire from a range of 200 yards from astern port quarter above with a long burst of cannon and machine-gun and saw chunks fly off the cockpit and engine. The e/a kept on course taking no evasive action; the pilot was evidently killed on the first burst. Morrison closed to fifty yards dead astern and slightly below and emptied his cannon and machine-gun on the e/a. The e/a was riddled like a sieve and the engine caught fire, pouring black and grey smoke. Oil covered Morrison's a/c and a piece of the port wing of the e/a, about three feet in diameter, hung down from the trailing edge near the tip. Morrison flew alongside and saw the pilot slumped forward on the stick. Morrison followed the e/a to the French coast and states he considered it a miracle that it continued to fly as it was so badly riddled with holes.

F/S Robert Reesor opened fire on the other FW-190 from a range of seventy-five yards from dead astern and slightly above. The e/a took no evasive action except to make a slight jink. Reesor emptied his guns from seventy-five yards and the pilot baled out at 15,000 feet. Reesor saw the pilot inflate his dinghy but was evidently too badly wounded to climb in. Reesor gave mayday from 7,000 feet and again from 1,000 feet and circled until the naval launch arrived. [Morrison had rejoined Reesor] off Beachy Head and made contact with the naval launch, which was about ten miles away, and guided the launch to the enemy pilot, effecting rescue. Morrison and Reesor landed at 1040 hours and received congratulations of all the pilots, ground crew and G/C Halling-Potts, the station commander.

September 9 Bob Reesor received from ASR the Mae West taken from the pilot he shot down, given to him as a souvenir. Written on it was: "Presented by Hans Schmidt, in appreciation of services rendered, to F/S R. Reesor." When ASR took him aboard they found him uninjured. As he spoke perfect English and thanked the rescue crew very much, they thought that he was an RAF pilot. Some time later one of the crew came up from below and said, "Sir, that bloke down below is a Fritz." So they took off all his clothes and mounted an armed guard. Bob hails from Pouce Coupe [B.C.] and the folks at home should be quite proud of his successful record.

September 12 Signal received advising P/O George Murray has been awarded the DFC. The CO phoned the message through to Gravesend where George is spending five days' leave. We bet the gal friend sews the ribbon on. Don Morrison, Scotty Murray and Bob Reesor make a hot team, not forgetting Stanley Cosburn. Rusty Bragg [engineering officer] says that after the war he is going to get himself a place on an island too small for an a/c to land, and off the beaten track of the air lanes so he will never hear or see the track of a kite.

September 22 Everybody busy around dispersal getting ready (packed) to move to Kenley, Surrey. In the evening the pilots of 401 and 133 and Biggin Hill headquarters went to a local and had a very enjoyable evening, shooting darts and stuff.

KENLEY, ENGLAND

September 24 Refuelling this morning was god-awful. The bowser went u/s and the pilots on readiness had to keep changing their 'chutes to other a/c.

September 26 [Three squadrons, 401, 133 and 64, escorted thirty-six bombers on a raid on Morlaix airfield on France's Brest peninsula.] The bombers were not seen until approximately sixty miles south of Brest [on the way home]. The Wing flew north for thirty minutes and it became evident that the wind at 24,000 feet was closer to 100 mph than the 34 mph reported by met [meteorological branch]. The bombers then saw land on the right and evidently thought they had reached the English coast at Falmouth and the bombers turned right. 133 and 64 Squadrons broke away from the formation and 133 went down to land. S/L Hodson knew it could not be England as water was seen to the north, so 401 kept course and height. R/T calls were then heard from 133 Squadron requesting positions as they had run into ack-ack fire. After the Wing had been airborne for 1½ hours, ops finally gave the position as 100 miles south of the English coast, and gave a homing vector of 020 degrees. Calls were then heard from 133 Squadron, some having been hit by a/a and some pilots out of petrol. 401 continued on course 020 which was later changed to 030 and seven of our a/c landed at Bolt Head at 1820 hours, and three landed at Harrowbeer at 1820. P/O L.E. Hokan, forty miles south of the English coast, reported, "Out of petrol, baling out, so-long boys, will see you tomorrow." He was last seen in a gradual dive and has not been picked up. S/P D. Wright missed the landing ground and crashed at Torquay and is in hospital seriously injured. S/L Hodson asked permission to do ASR but was not allowed. Until sighting the English coast on the return journey all pilots were of the opinion that they would have to bale out.

A full report covering this operation was prepared and submitted to Fighter Command Headquarters the following day. Of the twelve a/c of 133 Squadron, only one returned and this survivor made a crash landing in England after turning back due to engine trouble. [This was] probably the riskiest do the Squadron was ever on and it is evident that many casualties were avoided by clear thinking and cool behavior of all members of our Squadron when it looked as if all pilots would have to abandon their a/c. As P/O Hokan had used his auxiliary tank for ten or fifteen minutes on the run down from Kenley to Bolt Head and there were no facilities to refuel at Bolt Head, this accounts for him running short. He was a very keen type who is greatly missed by all.

It was long, long after the war before the British admitted they had lost an entire fighter squadron in France because of a bad wind forecast. The Germans captured most of the planes intact when they landed.

September 30 Jack Chapin received a letter from Leo Armstrong, prisoner of war. He states he is okay and quite well. He was blown ashore in his dinghy off Dieppe.

October 2 [F/L Morrison probably destroyed an ME-109 when the Squadron escorted forty-eight American bombers in a raid on an aircraft factory at Meaulte.] F/S Reesor failed to return and is listed as missing. Bob has been such a favorite with everyone in the Squadron. While only nineteeen years old, he proved himself a capable and aggressive pilot. In all his actions he exemplified the highest ideals of the RCAF.

October 5 On Blue Section formation practice, we regret to report the loss of P/O R.G. Riddell. The Section was pulling out of a dive at 7,000 feet. Blue 3 (Riddell) instead of pulling out continued down. Eyewitnesses [on the ground] state the aircraft was seen to dive at an angle of seventy degrees with motor running, making no effort to pull out, and crashed with a loud explosion 2½ miles north of Detling aerodrome near the village of Rainham. Investigation into the source of the accident is being conducted by the Air Ministry.

October 9 [F/L G.B. Murray and F/S E.L. Gimbel shared an FW-190 destroyed while escorting 108 Fortresses to Lille.] P/O Manley was fired upon by a Fortress from a range of 600 to 700 yards, two m/g bullets passing through the leading edge of the port wing.

October 20 It was a year ago today that 401 moved into 11 Group and to celebrate a party of thirty-two journeyed to the Greyhound Hotel, Croydon, and a very enjoyable time was had by all. P/O Bragg met an old friend from Calgary and [loaned] him £2. Unfortunately, the next morning he couldn't remember the friend's name.

November 3 An order came from 11 Group Headquarters stating that Spitfire IXs could henceforth be used on rhubarbs [low-level forays on ground targets], so the pilots spent most of the morning picking out routes. P/O Gimbel and F/L Grant were airborne on a rhubarb to attack an electrical and transformer station at Holque. They crossed the French coast three miles east of Gravelines and about three miles inland a locomotive was seen, attacked and damaged. Before the target was reached, F/L Grant's port wing was damaged in contact with a bird. [Both planes returned safely.]

November 8 [F/L Don Morrison and P/O D.R. Manley were missing after a Squadron combat with FW-190s over Dunkirk. F/L E.P. Wood reported he thought one FW-190 was shot down by Morrison and Manley together.]

Morrison, of Toronto, was returned to England in late 1943 in a repatriation of wounded prisoners of war. He had lost his left leg after being shot down in flames. He was unconscious for ten days in a Luftwaffe hospital, where he remained for a month before being moved to a prison camp in Germany. On repatriation, he wrote an article, distributed by The Canadian Press, about his experience. He said: "The truth about life in prison camp, although there's no specific complaint you can make, is that it's colorless and dreadfully monotonous. Every day is exactly the same and there is no future to look forward to except the distant future of the end of the war which, after a while, gets to be something completely unreal." Morrison had won both the DFM and DFC and his combat record showed 5⅓ German planes destroyed, four probably destroyed and four damaged. It was the highest individual score in the Squadron since the Battle of Britain.

November 16 The first of a series of talks on co-operation between the Army and Air Force was given by Major Stuart. [The pilots were given a brief outline of the part fighter pilots would be expected to play when the Second Front was established in France.]

November 28 The pilots spent the afternoon addressing their Christmas cards.

December 1 In changing formation P/O Livingston touched the propeller of F/O Ince and both a/c went into a spin at 1,500 feet. F/O Ince was able to regain control and landed safely on the aerodrome, the only damage being a bent propeller and cannon mounting. P/O Livingston nearly regained control and was straightening out in almost level flight when he crashed on the side of a hill two miles northwest of the aerodrome. He was assisted from the a/c by two civilians working nearby and taken to hospital where it was found he was suffering from back injuries and cuts and bruises about the head. It is expected he will recover in three weeks. The Spitfire caught fire and is a complete wreck. The names of the two civilians are being obtained and [they will be] suitably rewarded.

December 3 Air Vice Marshal Curtis visited the pilots' dispersal hut [and] spent a very enjoyable half-hour looking through the Squadron's scrapbook. A/V/M Curtis gave a short talk and broke the news that the Squadron was losing their Spitfire IXs, stating that it couldn't be avoided as there was a shortage in the East. All the pilots were feeling rather badly about it and would like to go to the East also.

December 4 The Wing had penetrated about ten miles inland [France] when Sgt B. Nickel went into a spin and is
thought to have crashed, as smoke was seen coming from a
spot on the ground shortly after. This was not a result of
enemy action and it is thought that Sgt Nickel must have
had some trouble with his oxygen supply, causing him to
black out, from which he never recovered. P/O J.W. Fiander and Sgt H.M. Batters were never seen [after a combat]
but ops room reported that they had both baled out over
the sea. P/O Fiander was later picked up by the ASR patrol
and taken to the naval hospital at Dover where it was found
he had been wounded in the left knee. A search was made
until dusk for Sgt Batters but without success.

Barbara Gardiner wrote to the Squadron December 27, 1942,
asking for the return of the belongings of Sgt Batters, who came
from Portage la Prairie, Manitoba. "You see," she wrote, "Hank
and I were to have been married on May 15th and it seems as if
the whole world has crashed."

December 8 A talk was given by S/P Navarro who had been
shot down in Germany thirteen months ago and had escaped and returned to England.

December 9 Two of the boys went to Dover via the Tiger
Moth to visit P/O Fiander who is recovering in the naval
hospital and took him his Christmas parcels.

December 11 [Two Spitfires] on patrol from Beachy Head to
Shoreham were vectored onto four FW-190s flying at 200
feet about four miles off the English coast at Hastings. P/O
Cosburn closed to 250 yards and fired at the one on the
right and observed strikes on the tail, rudder, fuselage and
wings. The FW-190s turned slightly to the right and Cosburn closed to 150 yards, firing the balance of his ammunition, observing further strikes, and the e/a slowed up
considerably and began to give off black smoke. This e/a
was seen to crash into the sea by Royal Observer Corps,

Hastings. F/O Ibbotson saw the other three FW-190s endeavoring to manoeuvre on the tail of Cosburn and turned toward them, forcing them to turn out to sea. He closed to 300 yards on the tail of the last one and delivered a four-second burst of cannon and observed a strike on the port wing.

December 25 At 0837 Red Section airborne on patrol Shoreham to Beachy Head. At 0936 Yellow Section airborne on patrol Shoreham to Beachy Head. At 1038 White Section airborne on patrol Shoreham to Beachy Head. At 1224, Squadron was released.

1943

THE WAR BEGAN TO turn in favor of the Allies. The British and Americans ran the Germans and Italians out of North Africa and the Canadian Army joined in the assault on Sicily and Italy in July. A Canadian wing flying from Tunisia participated in the softening-up campaign. The RCAF's No. 6 Bomber Group in England became operational and grew to fourteen from the original eight squadrons. No. 1 Squadron spent the early part of the year in Yorkshire out of the thick of things, but returned to the main scene of fighter action in the south early in the summer.

KENLEY, ENGLAND

January 15 Red 1 and 2 dove to attack [three locomotives] and Red 2 (P/O H.D. MacDonald) pulled out of the dive at 800 feet and attacked and damaged an engine by cannon fire about five miles west of Bayeux. Red 1 (S/P W.K. Ferguson) was last seen still in a dive at about 1,000 feet from which it is thought he never pulled out. Flak was seen being fired from one machine-gun position on the roof of a factory, but it is not thought that S/P Ferguson was hit.

January 17 P/O Gimbel saw two FW-190s above him. He got in a short attack on one during which the e/a descended from 7,000 to 3,000 feet. He failed to see the FW-190 hit the deck but its crash was observed by several other members of the Squadron.

January 20 F/O H.C. Godefroy and P/O MacDonald took off from Kenley at 1225 hours on a routine patrol from Beachy Head to Shoreham. Godefroy sighted a formation of thirty-plus FW-190s coming out over the Channel at zero feet from the hills west of Newhaven. He states: I climbed to 1,000 feet and attacked an FW-190 on the extreme left of the formation from dead astern. I fired all my ammunition from 300 yards and saw strikes all over the tail and mainplane. At first he weaved gently and then turned slightly to port. I pulled up and observed P/O MacDonald hitting another FW-190 and as there was an FW-190 on his tail I ordered him to break off. The FW-190 [attacked by Godefroy] was seen to crash into the sea by four witnesses, including the aerodrome airman of the watch and the duty pilot at Friston.

January 22 All ranks participated in a Squadron dinner and social evening at the new airmen's mess. 401 Squadron still proves to be made of good mixers, and all agreed it was the best feed for a long time. Seven kegs of ale were tapped, everyone freely treating everyone else. A group of policemen entertained in cabaret style, assisted by the station dance band. The evening degenerated nicely into song and speech-making. Inter-flight rivalry was short-lived with F/Ls Bitsy Grant and Scotty Murray, A and B flight commanders, embracing each other so all could see and applaud.

January 23 At 0730 hours the Squadron marched out of Kenley station and entrained for Catterick, where they arrived at 1625 hours. The airmen's quarters were found in a filthy condition, and in view of the fact that Kenley had been left spotless, the boys were feeling disgusted.

CATTERICK, ENGLAND

January 24 The fog was so thick that flying was impossible. The boys were on the job bright and early and spent the day unpacking and were ready to go operational by the end of the day. A detachment was sent to Thornaby, thirty miles away. Thornaby is badly overcrowded, Czechs and Poles swelling the normal population. Quarters are squalid and all ranks wasted no time getting out to reconnoitre the district, where night life abounds.

February 9 The dining room of The Angel witnessed the good fellowship of 401's officers and senior NCOs. S/L E.L. Neal [the new commanding officer], F/Ls Murray and Grant, F/O Bragg and P/O Cosburn all got up to voice pride and faith in our past and future as "the best darned outfit in England."

February 17 Three aircraft were airborne at 1355 hours for formation flying. At 1401 hours P/O Bishop, flying No. 3, reported by R/T that No. 1 and 2 (WO1 Muirhead [who had arrived on the Squadron the day before] and F/S L. Gilis) had collided at 6,000 feet. Later P/O Bishop said both a/c went into spins, neither pilot baling out before disappearing through cloud at 2,000 to 3,000 feet. The crash party found both a/c buried deeply in farmland, 1½ miles apart, about four miles south of Northallerton, with wreckage strewn across the fields between them. The pilots' bodies were not in the parts of the a/c showing above the ground.

February 18 Difficulty is being met keeping the Spitfires serviceable, many showing signs of age and requiring engine changes. In the afternoon, a party of the RAF Regiment was made available to commence digging for the bodies of WO1 Muirhead and F/S Gilis.

February 19 The body of WO1 Muirhead was recovered.

February 21 Attempts to recover F/S Gilis's body were abandoned as it lies fifteen to eighteen feet under the surface in soft sand.

March 4 P/O Fiander returned to the Squadron today from a long hospitalization and convalescence for a wounded leg, suffered December 4th, 1942, in a sweep over France.

March 5 In the evening a Squadron dance was held in the station cinema which in every way was a proud success. The event lasted from 2000 hours to midnight, and the WAAFs responded well to the general invitation issued to them. A well-stocked bar was well patronized. No untoward incident marred the evening.

April 1 Today was the twenty-fifth anniversary of the founding of the RAF, and after some a/c tests and formation low flying in the morning all pilots not on readiness were released for the day. A big anniversary dance was held in the sergeants' mess in the evening.

April 2 [A party was held] at the officers' mess. All drinks were free, the food plentiful and excellent, and a strenuous evening was enjoyed by nearly everyone. F/L G.B. Murray, DFC, was posted as an instructor to No. 61 OTU. He joined 401 in October 1941 as a sergeant and in nearly 100 trips over Hun-held territory proved his leadership and flying and fighting ability in such a way as to earn steady promotion. FW-190s exclusively have been his combat diet. He is credited with two destroyed, 1½ probably destroyed and 1½ damaged.

April 10 The Most Reverend Derwyn T. Owen, Archbishop of Toronto and Primate of the Church of England in Canada, visited the Squadron in the afternoon, spending some time at dispersal with personnel of the unit.

April 14 Leaving today was LAC J.A. L'Abbe on repatriation to Canada for a pilot's course. Jim, or Red, is one of the few remaining originals of the Squadron who came over in June 1940, leaving nine others of that hardy breed behind with us.

April 16 This being the first of the right nights of the April moon period, ten a/c were at thirty minutes' available all night. Pilots maintained their "availability" in their respective messes, and, later, their beds. No night flying was attempted.

April 25 At 2300 hours hi-jinks broke loose among the officers in the mess. With shirts outside trousers and ties about waists, an old-fashioned roughhouse was staged in the anteroom. Three absentees were summoned from bed and carried into the "inner sanctum" on their mattresses. There a couple of hours of roughhouse tactics took place, including horseback tilts, tumbling and an East versus West football scrimmage. Casualties were remarkably few and before the party broke up in the wee small hours, 401's mark had superseded that left by 403 Squadron on the ceiling of the ante-room.

April 26 The place was subdued as many a pilot nursed an aching joint as a result of last night's violent exercise.

April 27 The first of our Spitfires to have its wings clipped has come from the hangar and was flown today. The modification certainly detracts from the characteristic grace of the Spitfire's lines, but improved manoeuvrability is claimed as a result.

April 30 Forty-four members of the Squadron subscribed $3,000 in the Fourth Canadian Victory Loan drive which closed with the end of April. Enthusiasm for buying Victory bonds may be described as "abnormal" but reflects credit on such a large portion of the Squadron, about a third, who see fit to lay aside part of their savings or service pay in this way.

May 11 S/L E.L. Neal [commanding officer] received his DFC at the investiture at Buckingham Palace this morning and returned with F/L Grant by air from Debden, bringing the highly cherished DFC and new gramophone records.

May 22 Due to the heavy smoke haze there was no flying; even the birds walked.

May 27 A party was thrown in the officers' mess for 219 Squadron. Pillow fights, broken glass, feathers and casualties characterized the latter part of the evening. F/L Grant's visiting cousin collected a sprained ankle and black eye while [one pilot of 219] ended up in hospital with various sprained tendons. F/O "Wet Deck" Hamilton, playing Sir Galahad rescuing a fair damsel in distress, did a facial remodelling on F/O Jerry Denancrede, Squadron old-timer attached for a short stay with us. The more artistic element of the party meanwhile went to work, built human pyramids and left theirs and the Squadron's marks on the anteroom ceiling. Altogether, a quiet evening at home.

May 28 In the evening all ranks gathered at dispersal for a little "family" party. Several kegs of beer were opened and when emptied with dispatch the party came to a graceful close.

May 29 Despite the lack of operational activity, which tends to brown off a unit used to much more excitement, it is safe to say that all ranks in many ways have enjoyed their winter on the moors of Yorkshire's North Riding. Though the station is remote from civilized parts, the facilities provided for work and recreation were excellent. If social life was somewhat one-tracked, several romances budded among the ground crew. Most are agreed Catterick was a better place to hibernate than some we know.

REDHILL, ENGLAND

May 30 Redhill, Surrey, is cramped for ground crew [but] to be back on ops is an overriding compensation for most anything else.

June 5 Our future operations must necessarily be limited to low-level work such as close escorting of bombers, etc. Major Don Blakeslee, former 401 pilot, blew in today in his big Thunderbolt for a visit. He leads the American wing at Debden now and is soon to become a lieutenant-colonel.

June 6 F/O Bishop was flying in the neighborhood of the drome when his a/c caught fire. He first prepared to bale out, then decided to try to reach base. He made a wheels-down approach from the east but when about 100 yards short of the field he hit a row of trees which ripped off his undercarriage and he crashed in a farmer's field. His predicament was seen from dispersal and when the tender got near the crash discovered its way was barred by barbed wire and had to make a long detour. F/O Bishop had gotten clear of his a/c and, though shaken up, was unhurt — considered miraculous, especially as his harness was undone in preparation to jump. F/O Bishop has the real sympathy of his fellow pilots in the latest series of mishaps [two belly landings when the undercarriage wouldn't go down] he's suffered and hope his streak of fortune will turn for the better.

Arthur Bishop was the son of Canada's World War I ace, Billy Bishop. His bad luck made him the butt of a story in the RCAF at the time: "Bishop's record is five destroyed — two Hurricanes and three Spitfires." But the younger Bishop was as brave as his father and, as we shall see, achieved some success against the Germans. He survived, and wrote a marvellous book about his father, *The Courage of the Early Morning*.

June 17 P/O Swackhammer arrived with his crew to begin filming "High Flight," the story of the life of the Squadron. The script has been very tastefully prepared and should provide an interesting story as a short subject.

June 18 The RCAF film unit was recalled to London in view of our impending move, thus ending for the present our chances of "going Hollywood." [The move to Friston was cancelled.]

June 19 Our four remaining old originals, those inveterates who came overseas with the Squadron, were in a party of 100 such types from all over England celebrating their third anniversary in England at the Pavier Arms in London. G/C McNab, CO of the Squadron then, was present and the 401 representatives were F/O R.M. "Rusty" Bragg, engineering officer, F/Ss E.B. "Whizzer" White and W.C. "Gunner" Gunn, NCOs in charge of A and B flights respectively, and F/S J. "Jackson" Moffat, wireless NCO.

June 22 Our part in Ramrod 99 [a series of bombing raids] was that of escort cover to twelve Mitchells bombing the dock area at Rotterdam as first diversion to the U.S. 8th Air Force's first daylight raid on the Ruhr. All our a/c landed safely. Notification was received from the honorary secretary of the club that S/L Neal and F/O Fiander have been awarded life memberships in the "Goldfish Club — gold for the value of life, fish for the sea." Their badges arrived with the notification. S/L Neal went into the drink in May 1942 and F/O Fiander in December 1942.

June 26 A dozen barrels of beer and plenty of sandwiches kept the [party] going till a late hour. The CO said [midway through] that there was still lots of beer to be consumed and reminded all of a good Squadron motto: "We leave FA behind us."

July 19 [Over France] Yellow 1 (F/L Ormston) opened fire from 300 yards, thirty to thirty-five degrees deflection, with a four-second burst from cannon and m/g. Numerous strikes were seen on the e/a's [FW-190] cockpit and engine cowling. This concentrated fire is believed to have killed or incapacitated the pilot for no evasive action was taken, the e/a rolling on its back in a steep dive.

August 1 In the early morning word was received that F/L Ibbotson had died of internal injuries [from a motorcycle accident]. The Squadron is shocked and saddened at the loss of this able and popular young officer.

STAPLEHURST, ENGLAND

August 7 The boys are quite happy in the orchard, but find the lack of hot water rather a bind. An outdoor oven for hot soup, etc., has been started by a couple of enterprising pilots, and the [tent] encampment is beginning to look like home already.

September 18 At approximately 1010 hours, F/O J. W. Fiander, flying Blue 3, was forced to leave the formation due to a glycol leak at 14,000 feet a few miles north of Rouen. He glided the a/c with an idling engine out of the continent and baled out over the Channel from about 1,500 feet, approximately twenty miles west of the mouth of the Somme. He was picked up by a Walrus [plane] of ASR at 1115 hours and taxied to Dover, arriving at 2330.

September 19 F/O Fiander returned at lunch time. He may now claim a Bar to his Goldfish Medal.

September 26 At approximately 0930 F/L I.C. Ormston's engine packed up due to glycol failure at an altitude of 11,000 feet just off Dieppe. He glided over the Channel for approximately ten miles and baled out at 2,500 feet. Rescue was effected by ASR and he returned to the airfield around lunch time, none the worse for his dousing.

BIGGIN HILL, ENGLAND

October 15 F/S A.J. Edwards undershot the runaway in landing in a slight ground mist, ripping off the port mainplane and damaging the starboard mainplane. The fuselage was broken and the whole tail surface ripped off. He walked away from the crash after a bad shaking.

October 19 Duff weather precluded flying today and a release enabled most of the lads to look over the surrounding towns.

November 3 At 2130 hours the Squadron and about ten guests sat down to a [Thanksgiving] goose dinner with all the trimmings, including a session at the bar afterward. No casualties at this do!

November 23 The CO is now definitely sick with flu and he put himself to bed with bags of hot-water bottles, double whiskies and his wife's picture beside his bed.

November 26 F/L Sheppard got the first Hun since we've been on Spit IXs. Sheppard led his section down to the deck on a Jerry which had just taken off. After a five-minute chase, Sheppard destroyed the FW-190.

November 30 F/L MacDonald's engine cut out on him and he glided about halfway back to the English coast. About thirty miles from Bradwell Bay he intended to bale out but got stuck and went straight into the water. He has been listed as "missing, believed killed." He was a great fighter pilot with a good future, and it seems a pity that he had to go that way. Also missing from this operation is F/L Studholme. He also had engine trouble, and when his engine cut out he was last heard of over Holland, near the Dutch islands. It is hoped that he baled out safely. He was one of the Squadron's finest.

December 25 Minor Squadron formation beat-ups were practised over the aerodrome. The Squadron landed at 1045 and flying was ceased for the day to allow for Christmas Day services and, of course, celebrations. At 1100 hours we all went to the sergeants' mess as is the custom and had much to drink. F/L T. Koch, it seems, had reached the sergeants' bar long before the rest of us and he and Sgt Davis (one of the prettier WAAFs) were more or less two sheets to the wind before noon, and "Kocky" finally packed up about 1300 hours — out cold on his bed. The rest of the officers then went to the airmen's mess where we served the men with one of the finest meals one could wish for. A buffet lunch was served in the officers' mess and then the bar opened again and things really started. F/O W.T. (Grissle) Klersy and F/L J. Sheppard invaded the main mess and carried away one of the Christmas trees, which we were without in our mess. By late afternoon the pilots were feeling no pain and all the officers went down to the main mess for Christmas dinner. The meal was excellent and afterward things began to get quite lively. Nos. 411, 401 and 412 Squadrons had a verbal battle over the Tannoy system. F/O Klersy was the Squadron narrator and he began it all by announcing that he thought that 411 and 412 were deadbeats and asked if they had yet received their new supplies of bows and arrows. Several of the pilots left the camp early for private parties to which they had been invited, and the remainder attended the station dance. At this stage, F/O Klersy became unconscious and passed out for a few hours. "Kocky" had recovered consciousness by this time and was again in the running. In a few hours Grissle Klersy was again on his feet and going strong, so the night ended with all the pilots still on their feet, which I think is probably a record. [Boxing Day weather was too poor for flying, luckily.]

December 27   W/C K.L.B. Hodson gave the Wing a very severe lecture on accidents and the impression is now deeply
rooted in all that those who prang in any way have had it.
F/O Bishop was made dispersal officer (which duties he
promptly undertook by decorating the walls with female
forms).

December 28   It was around 1330 hours that a sad incident in
Squadron life took place. P/O R.W. Lawson and F/O F.B.
Evans found F/L D.F. Kelly dead in his bed. P/O Lawson
made the discovery and called F/O Evans. On examination,
it was found that F/L Kelly was shot through the head and
F/O Evans immediately called the medical officer. The
coroner's verdict on this death was that F/L Kelly had
taken his life while the balance of his mind was disturbed.
F/L Kelly had been in a very depressed state of mind because he had been posted from the Squadron and recommended for non-operational duties. A court of inquiry is
being held in the matter.

December 29   In the morning some of the pilots took sun-ray
treatment and for the remainder of the morning the CO had
everyone studying the geography of France.

1944

THE RUSSIANS DROVE THE Germans back toward Germany at fearful cost. The British, American and Canadian armies advanced slowly up the boot of Italy. The United States, Britain and Australia were pushing back the Japanese in the Far East. Finally, on June 6, the Allies launched their assault on Fortress Europe, landing on the north coast of France. No. 1 Squadron scored heavily against the German Luftwaffe in protecting the beachhead. It began operating out of France two weeks after the first landings and joined in the chase of the German army across France and into the Low Countries.

BIGGIN HILL, ENGLAND

January 1 The Squadron penetrated as far as Poix [on a fighter sweep] and came out over Le Tréport. This was New Year's night and a big dance was held in the main officers' mess. It was a good party with marvellous food, and was altogether a good ending for the holidays.

January 3 F/O Evans, one of the Squadron's oldest members, left sadly today to take up instructor's duties on a course at RAF Montrose.

January 4 The Squadron took part in Ramrod 418 to patrol Doulleus area while bombers bombed Noball targets [rocket gun emplacements].

January 6 The tow line pulling F/O R.K. Hayward's glider [one of three ferrying 412 ground crew north on exercise] parted and from 500 feet Hayward made a masterful swing back into the field — much to the relief of the erks he was carrying. In the meantime, the Squadron was on Ramrod 428, a fighter sweep while Mitchells and Mosquitos bombed Noball targets. The Squadron was attacked by an ME-109 and an FW-190. F/O H.K. Hamilton claimed the FW-190 as destroyed.

January 9 F/O Klersy and P/O Davenport took off on a rhubarb against Noball targets inland from Le Touquet. When about twenty-five miles inland, P/O Davenport's a/c was hit by flak. He and F/O Klersy climbed up into cloud, and then P/O Davenport reported that his engine had lost all power and that he was going to go down. F/O Klersy returned to base. This was a very unfortunate incident in that Tex Davenport was one of the most capable pilots and we will all miss him very much.

January 13 Word was received that F/L A.E. Studholme (missing 30-11-42) is a prisoner of war.

January 19 S/L Lorne Cameron [the commanding officer] made the brilliant suggestion that it was about time a dispersal party was held, and twelve cases of beer were procured from the officers' mess. Everyone brought down what food they had and poker and beer drinking ensued. In a game of red dog, F/O Roxy Heuser walked away with £45. Unfortunately, the Squadron had to do readiness all afternoon, which left some of us too sober. At night the party continued at the Bromley country club where a few blacks [faux pas] were put up — and it was hinted that if some of us didn't return again we would not be missed.

January 24 The weather was fair, and the Wing [401, 411 and 412 Squadrons] was airborne at 0915 on Ramrod 475 with fifty-four Marauders in the Le Tréport-Poix-Amiens area. The show was unexciting, except that when halfway between Boulogne and Dungeness, F/L J. Sheppard was seen gliding down toward the water. He had no R/T and his engine was dead. He began to lose height from 11,000 feet and at approximately 2,800 feet was seen to bale out. His descent was covered by the remainder of Yellow Section. F/O Hayward and F/O Klersy remained on the scene and sent F/L R.A. Haywood back to base. Klersy left, short of petrol, but met the Walrus [rescue plane] on the way back and guided it to the scene. F/O Klersy landed at

Flight Sergeant R.M. Zobell of 401 Squadron was wounded in the eye when his Spitfire was hit through rudder, wings, perspex and reflector sight while he was flying cover for the Canadian Army's Dieppe raid August 19, 1942. He got his plane back to base at Gravesend.

Flying Officers Ian Ormston and A.E. Harley at readiness beside a 401 Squadron Spitfire.

401 Squadron moved into the Normandy beachhead soon after the Allied landings June 6, 1944. Pilots on a Spitfire are, from the left: S/L Charles Trainor, the commanding officer, F/L G.W. Johnson, P/O Murray Havers, F/L William McRae, F/L Sandy Halcrow, F/O Gerry Bell, F/L Angus Morrison and F/L Cliff Wyman. Trainor was shot down and evaded capture only to be shot down again and taken prisoner.

Pilot Officer Hugh Godefroy, with friend. One canine mascot of 401 Squadron was taught to bark the correct number of times for air victories of the day. The Squadron scored as many as eighteen kills in one day. That's a lot of barking.

Canadian fighter wings had to help look after their own anti-aircraft defence in Normandy and afterward. The ground crew got the job. On 401 Squadron, there were some nervous challenges to frightened cows, which turned out to be friendly.

No. 1/401 battle honors. The badge is a Rocky Mountain sheep; the motto, "terribly swift death to the enemy." The squadron was the highest-scoring RCAF fighter squadron in the Second World War with 195$\frac{1}{2}$ enemy planes destroyed.

Hawkinge with only two gallons of petrol, which was a very good effort. F/L Sheppard was finally picked up by the ASR launch, the sea being too rough for the Walrus to land, after he had been in the water for about an hour. He was taken to Hawkinge where the CO later picked him up, quite well and thoroughly flushed with naval hospitality.

January 25 At night about half the Squadron went to the theatre to see the RCAF show called "Black-outs of 1943," which was very good indeed.

January 26 A dance was held in the gymnasium for the "Black-outs" show, which many of the pilots attended. It was probably the first time in a long while that many of us had danced with a Canadian girl, and a nice change.

February 5 F/O Hayward and P/O D.M. Wilson returned from leave, both looking a trifle the worse for wear.

February 9 Several of the pilots played a basketball game against Maintenance; they held their own for the first half, but lack of condition told in the last.

February 13 Those pilots not required for the show [bomber escort near Dieppe] went to London to see the Canadian-U.S. football game which the Canadians won by 16 to 6. All the game lacked was hot dogs and Coke.

February 14 [A Ranger operation was carried out by eight a/c of the Squadron.] F/O Hayward sighted an ME-210 taking off [from Chartres] and dove on it. He observed strikes and the a/c was seen to hit the ground and burst into flames. Two of the crew were seen to bale out very low but their parachutes failed to open.

February 24 Today's operation was a Fortress withdrawal, consisting of picking up the Fortresses and their heavy escort and bringing them out. This type of operation is getting to be a terrific bind to all the pilots and ground crews. With the number of escort fighters provided to the bombers these days, we can never expect to see a Hun come up to fight.

February 26   The officers gave a dance in the gym for the airmen. The building was decorated for the occasion and 100 WDs [RCAF Women's Division] from RCAF overseas headquarters were invited as partners for the boys. It was a most successful event.

February 29   In the evening several pilots went to the Hosking Arms at Oxted to a WLA [Women's Land Army] Leap Year dance, but none too many of us received any proposals.

March 3   [The Squadron] was airborne at 0835 as close escort for 108 Marauders bombing Laon aerodrome. The bombers were difficult to keep in formation but they were herded back. Just before we landed, two a/c of 412 Squadron collided on the runway and F/O Berryman was quite badly burned in the ensuing blaze.

March 7   [Over France] F/L Sheppard saw an FW-190 on the deck just over the perimeter track and went down on it with his section following. He engaged the Hun at treetop level and shot it down. As the Squadron was climbing back up, F/O Klersy spotted another FW-190 on the deck and went down. He had several good bursts from 200 to 100 yards and the Hun finally half-rolled into the ground in flames.

March 8   Our Squadron swept from Le Tréport to the outskirts of Paris. On the way out, everybody fired their guns at a barge and tug in the bend of the Seine near Duclan. These were set on fire and destroyed.

March 9   We had an accident near the drome when a glider, piloted by a 411 Squadron pilot, crashed in the valley. A few of us went out to the crash and how the pilot lived is a miracle. The lagging rope, which should have been released, caught in the trees and pulled the glider in nose first. P/O Mitchell suffered a broken leg.

March 10 F/L A.F. Jones, the new medical officer, arrived with his clever dog Dinghy, who is a cocker spaniel and has a very assorted set of tricks which include adding, subtracting and card tricks.

March 15 As we approached Cambrai aerodrome F/L Jack Sheppard reported Huns in the circuit with an ME-410 blocking the runway. The Squadron went down on these a/c and most of us had a good time. Sheppard destroyed one FW-190 with a one-second burst, F/O R.K. Hayward destroyed one FW-190, F/O D.D. Ashleigh destroyed one FW-190 and F/L A.F. Halcrow blew an FW-190 out of the air from such close range that his elevators were damaged from the debris. F/O Ashleigh's effort was particularly great in that this was only his fifth sweep. The fight lasted only a short while and the score came out four destroyed and two damaged with no losses for 401 except F/O Ray Sherk, who went down with engine trouble previous to the battle. There was as usual the RCAF Headquarters publicity department beginning their pestering and a radio broadcast and interviews took place in dispersal with the lucky pilots and some of the ground crew making recordings. Highlight of the interview was the efforts of Dinghy (our black cocker spaniel who belongs to F/L Jones) in barking out over the microphone the day's victories. The party continued for some time.

March 16 F/O K.B. Woodhouse reported engine failure [and baled out at 3,000 feet. As a result of this and other engine failures, the Wing was stood down while the cause was investigated.] Plugs were changed on several of the aircraft, but the authorities are still convinced that the failures were caused by the jettison tanks.

March 20 In the evening, some attended an ENSA [British Entertainments National Service Association] show which was lousy as usual and some played in a basketball game against the Army, which we won.

March 23 One JU-88 was shot down by F/L W.B. Needham of 412 Squadron. The Hun made a successful crash-landing and the crew scrambled to safety from the burning wreckage — or so they thought. F/L Needham then dove back down with his Brownings [machine-guns] blazing.

March 26 We received a great surprise when F/O K.B. Woodhouse walked into the dispersal after having escaped from France when he baled out southeast of Amiens on 16th March. This is considered a damn good show and Woody is going back to Canada for a month's leave.

April 1 Everyone packed up and dispersed to wash up and get into town to collect their girls for a Squadron party. The party started at 7:30 p.m. in the White Hart and after drinks dinner began at 8:15. This was probably one of the finest thrashes we have had for some time and novelty dances with inviting prizes gave it that extra touch. Most of the pilots had rooms for themselves and the girls in the Bromley Court. The next morning, drinking continued until past noon when F/O W.T. (Grissle) Klersy pulled off another performance when he captured a chicken in the backyard and climbed in through the window, triumphantly carrying the squawking pullet through the lounge.

April 2 Weather was too duff for flying and most of the pilots spent the day in town continuing with the party of the night before. At night several of us met in the New Bromley Club, which was the final phase of the party.

April 10 [The Squadron spent a week at Fairwood Common, Wales, for gunnery, bombing and strafing practice.] A security lecture was given to all officers by the Station CO on strict censorship of letters, etc. [The Squadron then moved to Tangmere and lived under canvas in preparation for a shift to the Normandy beachhead soon after the Allied invasion of Europe.]

TANGMERE, ENGLAND

April 18 We were very glad to see F/O R.M. (Tex) Davenport back from his escape from France.

April 19 F/L Scotty Murray could not release his bomb nor rack out over the sea on this do [raid near St. Pol, France] and after much effort was forced to abandon his a/c over Beachy Head. Scotty made a successful jump except for a sprained ankle. The a/c crashed but the bomb did not explode.

April 24 P/O T.W. Dowbiggin spotted an ME-110 which he attacked, and it burst into flames and crashed and exploded on the ground. The remainder of the trip was uneventful.

April 27 The Squadron was airborne at 1215 to dive bomb a railway bridge. F/O W.E. Cummings did not recover from the dive after releasing his bomb, and was last seen diving past the vertical, apparently out of control.

April 30 F/O G.D. Billing nearly flew straight into the target. After trimming his a/c in the dive, it bunted, as did F/O Cummings's, and after dropping his bomb all attempts to pull out proved futile. Just when he had given up hope of recovery, he wound on full right rudder and the a/c came out in a tight diving turn only a hundred-odd feet from the ground, so close that he flew right through the debris from the bomb-bursts.

May 7 [Near Laon] P/O Dowbiggin's jettison tank ran out and he was unable to restart his a/c. He was seen to make a beautiful forced landing and leave his a/c for the shelter of a nearby wood. S/L L.M. Cameron then went down and destroyed the a/c by cannon fire.

May 20 This Ranger was to sweep the Laon-Chievres-Cambrai area. Nearly all the pilots saw the Vimy Ridge memorial and commented on how it stood out shining against the dark background. The operation was without event.

May 21 The Doc found that most of us were behind in our inoculations and held a mass stabbing. Most of us had several shots with vaccinations as well, and [we played] cards to see who the unfortunate victims would be on readiness at dawn the next day.

May 26 Air Marshal Leigh-Mallory arrived and gave us a short address, stressing the importance of the part the Air Force would play in the coming operations.

June 3 When about twenty miles after crossing out [from France] F/O C.B. Cohen called up that his engine was quitting and he began to lose height. He apparently left baling out till too late, as his 'chute did not open. We circled the spot for half an hour but nothing was seen but the dye from his Mae West.

The CO and the Doc and a few pilots went to visit P/O Hubbard who is progressing favorably. His injuries are now listed as third-degree burns on his legs, and second-degree on his hands and face, as well as cuts and bruises on his face. Instructions came through to mark the a/c with black and white stripes from the wing roots to the ailerons and wireless mast to tail. We are not to go within twenty miles of enemy coasts with these markings on ops and must stay within our own coast on practice flying.

June 4 P/O C.F. Armstrong taxied into a sodium flare on the way out to the first patrol and smashed his prop. A request was submitted for his posting in the afternoon.

June 5   At 1745 the Squadron was sent off to patrol shipping off the Isle of Wight. The type and quantity of shipping seen suggested that D-Day was not far off. At 2330 all pilots gathered in our mess tent and G/C [W.R. (Iron Bill)] MacBrien told us that June 6th was D-Day and that the operation was already under way with paratroop landings on the beaches north of Caen. We were briefed for our part in the show which, for the first few days, was to be patrolling the beaches at 3,000 to 4,000 feet while the Americans did high cover and penetrations. Heavy bombers were on their way out as we were being briefed. It was 0130 hours when the pilots finally got to bed and their rising time was 0315.

June 6   Early morning was very cold with scattered showers and low cumulus. We were up at 0315, breakfasted at 0345 and set up on readiness at 0430. The Squadron carried out four patrols throughout the day, all over the beachhead. On the last patrol in the evening one thing of interest was the glow in the sky as Caen burned in the gathering darkness.

June 7   Sandwiches and tea were brought to us while we waited [at 0630] for first briefing. The Squadron carried out a patrol at 0810 and nearly became entangled with balloons flying in cloud at 2,000 feet near St. Aubin. The ground behind the beach near St. Aubin was littered with supply parachutes and gliders from last evening's airborne reinforcements. A JU-88 hit a balloon cable and crashed near the beach. At least a dozen JU-88s suddenly appeared out of cloud, some managing to dive at the beaches, the rest turning as we attacked and attempting to reach cloud. S/L Cameron called for everyone to pick his own target and the Squadron broke up. A melee ensued [and] the score at the end was F/L G. B. Murray and F/O W.A. Bishop shared one JU-88, S/L Cameron two destroyed, F/L R.H. Cull, one destroyed, F/O G.D. Billing, one destroyed, F/O D.F. Husband, one destroyed and F/L A.F. Halcrow, one probably destroyed, which evaded on fire with Thunderbolts chasing it. During the chase S/L Cameron passed over Caen town and aerodrome which is still very much in enemy hands, judging from the flak which came up. Return fire from the JU-88 sent a bullet through the perspex behind F/L Halcrow's head.

On the second patrol, the Squadron immediately on arrival over the beachhead spotted six-plus FW-190s approaching fast at a shallow angle from Le Havre direction. The Squadron split up, but the first section of FW-190s had already released their bombs. F/O W.T. Klersy destroyed one FW-190. P/O N. Marshall is believed to have been hit by flak, and he is listed as missing.

On the last patrol over the beachhead no enemy aircraft were seen, but intense flak from Caen and our own balloons flying in the dusk made the trip interesting.

June 8 At 1815 the Squadron carried out another patrol over Gold beach. The only interesting part of it was the terrific bombardment the Navy was giving to Hun installations near the coast. Fires could be seen dotting the battle area.

June 9 The weather was completely u/s, raining and blowing. The pilots spent the whole day [on standby] in the mess. No. 127 Wing took off at 2000 hours in very unfavorable weather to patrol the beachhead, but were met with considerable ack-ack from our own ships, and after several attempts to pass they were forced to return, having lost one pilot, another wounded, and six aircraft damaged.

June 10 We had hoped to be the first Canadian squadron to land in France, but No. 144 Airfield had landed on the same strip earlier in the day. As a consolation, we were the first Squadron in [our] Wing to land [to refuel].

June 13 F/L Johnson flew to France and returned later in the evening, but this was not operational as his jet tank was filled with beer for the thirsty advance party of No. 126 Wing Headquarters.

June 14 At 1315 hours 412 and our Squadron carried out a sweep in the Le Mans-Chartres-Evreux area. Considerable enemy transport was shot up. F/L Bouskill was forced to land on our strip in France on running short of petrol, got caught in some loose dirt, swung into two soldiers, killing one and seriously injuring the other, then dug in a wing tip. The aircraft was a complete write-off but F/L Bouskill was unhurt.

June 16 During the night there were three alerts and apparently the Hun has started using his long-awaited glider-bomb. F/L Bouskill arrived from France in an American landing craft.

BENY-SUR-MER, FRANCE

June 18 At 1400 hours the ground crew embarked in Dakotas to fly to France. The Squadron of twelve aircraft took off at 1900 hours to land at their new home [B-4 airstrip, Beny-sur-mer, and] proceeded to dig in for the night.

June 19 A ground and sea fog covered the airfield and in the afternoon it started to rain. This gave the boys a chance to dig their "funk-holes." They found from the first night's experience that there was a lot of noise and spent flak throughout the night, with the enemy trying to bomb the ships, and holes started appearing in the floors of the tents. Lined with matting and boarded over, the trenches proved quite a comfortable way of warding off any metal which might otherwise dent one's skull. Scrounging parties went out to a wrecked German radar station and quantities of wood and timber were obtained for slit-trench building. The airfield itself, though very dusty, is quite fair and everyone manages to cope quite well on landing. Take-off will be made in pairs because the amount of dust churned up is terrific. Bar and mess are functioning normally. Meals don't provide much variety since they all come from tins, but new potatoes and fresh green peas make them quite tasty, and with the appetite one develops in the open air all day, there are no complaints to be heard. Bread is the only thing that is missed, and "dog-biscuits" are not a very good substitute. Russ McLeod of the Canadian Legion is doing a good job and already has his portable cinema going in one of our large tents.

June 20 In the afternoon a party of eight pilots went into Bayeux, sampled some of the local steaks and wine and brought back a couple of bottles for the mess. There was the usual night activity but the clouds hid the fireworks display and there was nothing of particular interest to record.

June 21 When Red Section was flying just south of Bayeux, they met heavy flak from our own guns and were forced to go into cloud and on reforming F/O H.E. Fenwick could not be found. We learned later that he had been chasing a Hun which was being fired at by our own [anti-aircraft] gunners and had been shot down himself instead. He crashed with his a/c and was killed.

June 22 [We were] to bomb two bridges. As no direct hits were scored both bridges appeared to be standing when we left. At 2130 hours a very informal funeral was held for F/O Fenwick without a firing party. S/L Forbes officiated. The cemetery is a small plot just outside the camp area where several other Canadians are already buried. Following the funeral we were brought back to immediate readiness.

June 24 The Squadron was scrambled at 0600 hours to do an armed recce [reconnaissance] of roads in the Falaise-Lisieux areas. Several individual transports were successfully attacked. F/O Davenport flew to Tangmere at noon and returned later in the day with a few loaves of very welcome bread, and newspapers.

June 25 Another beach patrol was carried out by twelve aircraft which again was uneventful although several Mustangs and Thunderbolts were chased in the hope it was a Jerry, but no luck.

June 28 A four-man patrol was airborne at 0910 hours. Twenty FW-190s with a top cover of the same number of ME-109s was encountered south of Caen. During the combat that followed two FW-190s were destroyed for no loss. At 2115 we were sent out on an armed recce. While strafing transport south of Caen we were bounced by twelve FW-190s and a real dogfight started. After it was over we had destroyed four of the enemy a/c but had lost two. One pilot, however, was seen to bale out.

July 1 F/O G.D. Billing was hit by enemy flak seven miles south of Carentan but managed to crash-land safely in enemy territory. He was seen to leave his a/c and start running.

July 2 The Squadron did a sweep looking for transport but instead sighted and attacked about twenty-four FW-190s and ME-109s circling east of Caen at 14,000 feet. In the combat that followed F/L I.F. Kennedy destroyed one ME-109 and F/O Klersy destroyed another. F/L Kennedy's guns jammed after he had hit the Hun badly but he flew alongside the Jerry as he went in to crash. The enemy pilot waved frantically that he was through and had to crash-land. He evidently thought he was going to receive a finishing touch. On crashing into a field the enemy kite was smashed completely.

July 3 S/L Cameron was hit in the engine by flak and was forced to crash-land in a field north of Falaise. He was seen to land and get away from the aircraft. [Kennedy replaced Cameron as CO.]

July 7 F/O A.L. Sinclair chased three ME-109s in and out of the clouds and one of them finally half-rolled into the deck without apparently having been hit. Sinclair was then attacked by an FW-190 which he in turn set on fire. He landed at base rather short of petrol. Our final figures for the day show seventy-six sorties, 77.20 hours flown and four aircraft destroyed and one damaged.

July 10 We heard that Caen had fallen at last. The sound of gunfire from this section of the front has almost ceased.

July 12 The pilots spent the day [off] getting sunburned and collecting souvenirs from the front. The number of Jerry motor bikes in the Squadron is growing.

July 15 We were working with a new controller today and the confusion resulting, especially with new call signs also going into effect, was terrific.

July 18 Early morning marked the beginning of the big push east and south of Caen and the Squadron was airborne at 0540 hours using long-range tanks to patrol east of Caen while heavy and light bombers hammered German concentrations ahead of our advance. The expected enemy opposition did not materialize and there was very little flak seen, so when the Squadron landed at 0740 hours the pilots had nothing to report.

July 19 WO M.H. Havers has now become P/O Havers and the other pilots were very sorry that owing to the shortage of drinks he was unable to accept our good wishes over a glass of his whisky.

July 20 About three miles south [of Argentan] four FW-190s were seen and attacked. F/L R.M. Stayner caught one which he shot down into some woods. The pilot managed to bale out. F/L Stayner's victory was 401 Squadron's 100th since it was formed.

July 24 F/L W.R. Tew was hit by enemy flak and was last heard of at about 2,000 feet saying he was going to bale out. Due to heavy flak and poor visibility, he was not seen to do so.

July 26 Just over Dreux aerodrome, S/L I.F. Kennedy, DFC, CO of the Squadron, was hit by enemy flak in the engine and was forced to bale out a few miles further on. He was seen to land safely near a small wood. In the evening [it was] announced that F/L H.C. Trainor, DFC, was to take S/L Kennedy's place as CO.

July 27 A lovely day and a great start for the Squadron under its new management. On the return leg, just southeast of Caen, the Squadron closed with about fifteen ME-109s and FW-190s. A real dogfight followed and the Squadron did itself proud. Seven ME-109s were destroyed and one FW-190. The victors were S/L Trainor, F/L G.W. Johnson, F/L A.L. Halcrow, F/L W.R. McRae, P/O H.M. Havers, F/O G.A. Bell, F/O C.P. Wyman. Each destroyed one ME-109. F/L A.F. Morrison destroyed an FW-190. [Later] a patrol of six aircraft at 1840 hours ran into about twelve FW-190s southeast of Caen again. F/L R.R. Bouskill destroyed one. The others dived for the deck and escaped.

July 31 Near Domfront twelve FW-190s were spotted and attacked. F/L Klersy picked one off which crashed in flames. S/L Trainor also destroyed one. F/L T.P. Jarvis was shot down and his plane seen to crash. The Squadron landed at 1335 hours.

In this busy period air victories earned only a routine mention in the log. The Squadron was also engaged in bombing and strafing tanks and other ground armament as well as with its high- and low-level patrolling.

August 3 South of Domfront the Squadron ran into twelve ME-109s. F/Ls Johnson, Bouskill and R.H. Cull each destroyed one. The remainder managed to escape.

August 4 Twelve aircraft took off on an armed recce in the Falaise-Alençon area. Scattered transport was seen and attacked and the Squadron netted seven flamers, three smokers and seven damaged. Also, three soldiers on bikes were shot up.

B-18, CRISTOT, FRANCE

August 8 The Wing moved to its new strip at Cristot, B-18. At 1530 hours the new strip was operational. There are no towns of any size close to us so our stay here should on the whole be quite quiet.

August 13 During the afternoon the patrol did ASR work and succeeded in locating a dinghy with two or three men in it about fifteen miles south of Ouistram. Their position was given to the controller and it is hoped that they were picked up. S/L Sheppard, an old 401 flight commander and now CO of 412 Squadron, returned to the Wing today after escaping through the enemy lines when he was shot down on August 2nd.

August 14 F/L Murray returned today after escaping through the enemy lines. He was shot down on the 28th of June. While he was in hiding he met our former CO, S/L L.M. Cameron, in the hayloft of a barn. S/L Cameron was reported missing on July 3. High hopes are held that we'll be seeing him one day soon, too.

August 15 Transport is appearing plentiful as Jerry tries to escape to the Seine. There seem to be thousands of so-called ambulances on the roads and it's surprising how fast the "wounded" can run when our a/c fly low over them.

August 18 All operations were armed recces against enemy transport fleeing from the Falaise pocket. The Squadron flew six operations in all, totalling fifty-three sorties. Our CO, S/L H.C. Trainor, and F/O C.E. Fairfield were both hit by enemy flak on the first operation. F/O Fairfield was seen to crash and is reported as missing, believed killed. S/L Trainor was last seen flying south to try to make American lines. F/O R.M. Davenport was also hit by flak but managed to crash-land behind our lines and reported back to the Squadron the same day. The total score in transport for the day for the Squadron was sixty-one flamers, forty-four smokers and sixty-two damaged.

August 19 On the first operation of the day the Squadron ran into forty-plus FW-190s and ME-109s just east of Bernay. The twelve aircraft of our Squadron broke into them and during the combat F/L G.W. Johnson destroyed and damaged two FW-190s while F/L J.C. Lee also destroyed one FW-190. The German pilot went over the side and landed near his burning a/c. The Squadron suffered no loss.

August 20 About twenty-plus e/a were contacted and attacked. F/O R.M. Davenport destroyed and damaged two FW-190s while F/O D.F. Husband destroyed another. The Squadron suffered no loss. Time up 1917 hours and down at 2030 hours. Still no word of S/L Trainor but we are hoping he is with one of our advance army units and unable to get back at the moment.

August 23 Five of our a/c had to return early due to mud in their radiators from the muddy runways.

August 24 F/L Tew was reported safe with American troops. He was reported missing July 24. S/L I.F. Kennedy, our former CO who was reported missing July 26, walked into camp. There was much rejoicing on the return of these men, who will now probably return to Canada for a rest.

The Squadron has still two squadron leaders to hear from yet.

August 25 Just about supper time the much-hoped-for event happened when S/L Trainor returned to the field. He intends to take his ordinary leave and return to the Squadron. In the evening the officers' mess threw a dance to which 100 Canadian nurses were invited. There were numerous other guests. There were also numerous Maquis [French resistance fighters] dressed very well for the occasion. The affair was a great success.

The Squadron moved September 1 from B-18 to Evreux, to St. André the next day and to Poix the day after that.

POIX, FRANCE

September 3 The Army was moving so fast that St. André was still too far behind the front lines. The ground crew enjoyed themselves immensely during these moves. They have been seeing a great deal of France and its inhabitants. The road has led through many blasted towns and villages and it seemed rather strange that the people will still smile and wave at us even though their homes have been demolished. We have also seen the results of our strafing of enemy transport. German motor transport vehicles by the score litter the fields along the highway. Knocked out enemy tanks and armored vehicles as well as some of our own were also seen.

September 5 Duff weather prevented any operations, so the pilots investigated the neighboring towns in any kind of wheeled vehicle that could be found.

BRUSSELS, BELGIUM

September 7 Our new site is by far the most comfortable we have had yet in Europe. The officers' mess was practically undamaged and there were even enough billets left standing to house most of the ground crew. The people of Brussels lined the streets as the convoys moved through so the airmen had quite a time receiving and giving gifts and shouting back greetings.

September 10 This is a very busy aerodrome with almost every conceivable kind of a/c using it. Allied bombers and fighters are finding it very handy for an emergency landing after being damaged by enemy fighters or flak.

September 12 Numerous Dakotas are now using the field to bring in supplies of petrol and other essential items.

September 13 The Squadron was released at noon for twenty-four hours. Everyone streamed into Brussels for the night. Hot baths, ice cream, wine, women and song seemed to be the general trend. We are certainly piling up some operational hours in town — a very marvellous city and Canadians are treated like kings. It will be a very sorry day when we have to move.

September 14 The food has improved greatly in the last few days, even to the great length of having an egg for breakfast.

September 16 F/L Klersy left for England at noon. We are all sorry to see Bill go but he has completed a 260-hour tour and certainly deserved a rest. Lt/Cmdr A.C. Wallace, Royal Navy, is now attached to us to gain experience on Spitfires.

September 17 The Squadron along with all of the Wing was CB [confined to barracks] tonight due to impending operations. There is still some doubt whether we will move for a few days. The prospect of moving back into a tent at this time of year is none too inviting.

September 19 S/L Trainor's engine failed and he glided about 20 miles before he baled out near Derwen. The boys followed him down to about 500 feet but due to poor visibility because of ground mist, lost sight of him at that height. Derwen may or may not be near our lines, we can't tell for sure. F/L G.W. Johnson will take over the Squadron until the boss returns or another S/L is appointed.

LE CULOT, BELGIUM

September 21 We moved to our new airfield at Le Culot at noon today. There is a cement strip at this drome and although the field is a little crowded with 137 Wing also being here, the approach to the strip is the best yet. We are living in barracks which are as yet in an unfinished state. However, they are better than tents. There seems to be a bountiful supply of eggs and fruit in the area and everyone is taking full advantage of it. S/L Trainor hasn't been heard from yet but he walked out before and everyone is quite confident that he can repeat the performance.

September 22 From an operational standpoint the fighter sweep [near Arnhem] was uneventful. However, on the way home, F/O J.N.G. Dick collided with Lt/Cmdr A.C. Wallace, who went into an inverted spin and plunged straight in. F/O Dick made a forced landing and is reported shaken up but uninjured.

September 23 The body of Lt/Cmdr Wallace was brought back from B-66 [airfield] and will be buried in Brussels tomorrow afternoon. Pilots from the Squadron will act as pallbearers.

September 24 We heard unofficially through the underground that S/L Trainor is a prisoner of war.

September 25 Twelve a/c took off to intercept enemy a/c trying to bomb the Nijmegen and Arnhem bridges. The Squadron ran into thirty-plus FW-190s and ME-109s and engaged them. When the dogfight was over, F/L Bouskill had shot down one FW-190 and damaged one ME-109. F/L

G.W. Johnson brought his total up to eight destroyed and four damaged by shooting down two ME-109s and damaging another. F/O G. Hutchings was shot up so bad he had to land at Eindhoven along with Johnson and Bouskill, who had run short of fuel.

September 26 Because of heavy rain during the night the runway was again u/s this morning. All pilots plunged in to help fill in some of the holes with pick and shovel. They managed to have it serviceable by eleven o'clock. We carried out three high patrols, all uneventful.

September 27 Today the Wing shot down more enemy a/c in one day than ever before, the score being twenty-two a/c destroyed and ten damaged. Unfortunately, 401 Squadron was unable to contribute any. The Squadron flew three low-level patrols in the same area as the other Squadrons [411 and 412] but outside of being bounced once by two ME-262s [the new German jet fighter] which flew off and could not be engaged, all patrols proved uneventful. Some of our pilots were wild at not being able to contact anything.

September 29 S/L R.I.A. Smith [the new CO, from 412 Squadron] was leading the Squadron and led them right into a dogfight with thirty-plus ME-109s and FW-190s. After the fight was over we had tallied up a very nice score of nine ME-109s destroyed, four ME-109s damaged and one FW-190 damaged. F/O Hutchings failed to return and is listed as missing. [S/L Smith, F/L H.J. Everard, F/O J.C. Hughes and F/O Husband each destroyed two and F/L Bouskill one.] A good example of the ferocity of the scrap is contained in F/L Everard's second claim of an ME-109 destroyed. It reads as follows: The second dogfight began immediately the first finished, the victim being the a/c nearest me in the remainder of the formation who still milled about on the deck. I gave this a/c two two-second bursts from seventy-five yards quarter astern. On the second burst it exploded and I was unable to steer clear of the debris. Part of the pilot's body hit my mainplane inboard of the starboard cannon and dented it. Superficial damage to the a/c.

October 1   F/L L.W. Woods arrived today to join the Squadron. He makes the fifth new face in two days. Many of the original D-Day Squadron are already back in England or on the last few hours of their tour.

October 2   Over the [Nijmegen] bridge area we bounced four FW-190s but in turn were bounced by another four e/a. W/O M. Thomas was shot up and had to bale out, landing safely behind our lines. F/L Bouskill failed to return. No one saw him go down so it is hoped that he landed safely some place.

B-84 STRIP, NETHERLANDS

October 3   Our Squadron was lucky enough to acquire the use of a new dry loft in a barn about three miles from our dispersal. At present it is being used by some officers of an armored division but they are willingly sharing it with us. We find the climate much more damp and cold here and everyone sleeps with extra clothing on.

October 4   What a change this is from Belgium. Everyone here is usually in bed and asleep by nine o'clock. The nearest town is about twenty miles away and offers very little in the way of entertainment.

October 5   Twelve a/c took off and while on patrol one ME-262 was spotted diving toward Nijmegen. The Squadron promptly dived after it and after a chase during which five members of the Squadron took a squirt at it, the e/a started to burn in the air and finally crashed on friendly territory. The five members were S/L Smith, F/L Everard, F/L Davenport, F/O J. MacKay and F/O A.L. Sinclair. This ME-262 shot down today is the first one destroyed by either the RCAF or RAF.

October 9 Again no flying due to weather. Knock-rummy games are holding sway in the mess. Some of the pilots and airmen are getting the opportunity to visit the Army toward the front lines.

October 10 The rains have come and from the looks of things the little Dutch boy must have taken his finger out of the hole in the dyke. The strip is u/s and everything is floating in an oozing sea of black mud.

October 11 The pilots are still making pilgrimages to the front lines for excitement and to the nearest towns for baths.

B-80, VOLKEL, NETHERLANDS

October 14 The Squadron was billeted in a village school three miles from the drome.

October 15 The Squadron started off hammer and tongs on their long-delayed rail interdiction program. Most of the pilots were pretty rusty and those who weren't were totally inexperienced.

October 17 Pilots saw the latest combat films in the mess, including the ME-262 film which came out of 401's cameras.

October 23 S/L R.I.A. Smith, F/L G.W. Johnson and F/L W.T. Klersy all received Bars to their DFCs.

The Squadron spent the next ten days on an air firing course at Warmwell, England, returning to B-80 November 4. The diary noted: "The Squadron spent the last six days of this month [October] doing air firing, dive bombing and extensive operations in London, Bournemouth and Weymouth. The exact details of these operations are unknown, but it is presumed that a few great air battles were once again fought over many an English pint."

November 8 We received word that His Majesty the King has approved our Squadron crest, A Ram's Head, the motto being "Very Swift Death to our Enemies."

November 11 No e/a are being sighted on these shows [railway bombing] but the accuracy and the density of the flak is terrific.

November 13 The whole area here has become a sea of black mud and some tents have been flooded out. Rumor has it that by December we should be in winter quarters.

November 20 A Tempest aircraft from 122 Wing had its engine cut just after take-off and tried to make a forced landing. Approaching the field he was thrown off course by a heavy gust of wind and ploughed into one of our aircraft which was just on the verge of taxiing out onto the runway. The Tempest just chewed through the Spitfire, killing the airman on the tail, LAC R.L. (Joe) Butler.

November 21 The highlight of the day was the shooting down of the 200th Hun by the Wing since its formation. The big problem which caused much debate was the fact that both 401 Squadron and 411 Squadron engaged e/a at the same time and each claimed one FW-190 destroyed. Since the intelligence section had offered a trophy to the pilot who shot down the 200th, the problem became more and more difficult. However, G/C McGregor, the Wing CO, simplified things by putting up another trophy so now all that was left to be straightened out was whether F/L W.C. Connell or F/L E.B. Sheehy destroyed the a/c [claimed by 401]. Both pilots had a squirt at it, F/L Sheehy finally finishing it off.

November 22 The CO, S/L Smith, and officers and men from 401 attended the funeral of LAC Butler, who was buried near Heide at 1030 hours.

November 24 No sorties flown for three days and all tent dwellers spent most of their time attempting to stem the flood of water which has been rapidly gaining in the last twenty-four hours. An issue of rum helped to ease the situation and take away some of the chill. [S/L Smith completed two tours and was replaced by S/L Everard.]

B-88, HEESCH, NETHERLANDS

December 6 Aircraft landed at the new strip without mishap. Conditions were better than many expected — a real roof and a proper floor underfoot perked everyone up considerably.

December 14 We found out today that the Squadron had been adopted by one of the earliest RCAF stations, No. 2 SFTS [Service Flying Training School], Uplands, Ottawa. Already a great many generous parcels have arrived and the food and cigarettes have been more than welcome.

December 17 At 1040 the first section was scrambled as Huns were reported in the area. A few seconds later, five ME-109s shot across the drome; one of them actually took the time to bank from side to side, possibly endeavoring to identify the drome — as if they didn't already know where we were. An interesting point in station activities is the noticeable number of V1s [buzz bombs] which pass over. B-88 seems to be on a direct line between the launching sites and the German targets in Holland.

December 23 401 are holding their traditional Christmas party for the airmen tonight and, if the liquor supply is any indication, there should be a few u/s bodies around the camp. F/L A.L. Sinclair, P/O H.D. Clarke and F/L K.L. Magee were injured in an automobile accident early this morning and are in hospital in Eindhoven. [Sinclair and Clarke were later transferred to hospital in England.]

December 24   After last evening's party both pilots and ground crew were right on their toes and eager to get into the morning's work. The Squadron did two shows, one in the morning and one in the afternoon. Both proved uneventful.

December 25   The Squadron flew thirty-six sorties and shot down two ME-109s just to help everyone's Christmas spirit along. F/L Johnnie MacKay destroyed one which crashed on fire in the suburbs of Duisberg while F/S A.K. Woodill, a new member of the Squadron, and F/L Bud Connell shared the second. An unfortunate incident marred the day. S/L Everard failed to return off the second show. It is thought that during the engagement with the ME-109s his a/c was hit by some debris from the e/a and he was forced to bale out somewhere south of Venlo.

December 29   F/L Paddy Sheehy was lost during the scrap with twenty FW-190s and ME-109s which bounced the Squadron. His a/c was last seen going down in flames and although a parachute was seen floating there is little hope that it was his. F/O G.D. Cameron [acting CO] and F/O F.T. (Freddie) Murray each destroyed an FW-190. Still no word on S/L Everard.

December 31   Returning from the last show, W/O M. Thomas spotted an adventurous buzz bomb flying through our circuit and diving on it gave the airfield a first-class exhibition of air firing by picking it off in full view of everyone. It exploded harmlessly in a field a few miles southwest of our strip.

1945

THERE WAS HARD FIGHTING until the Allies crossed the Rhine into Germany and met the Russian armies on the Elbe River. Germany surrendered May 8. No. 1 Squadron operated in close support of the ground forces; in one day near the end of the war it shot down eighteen German planes. Japan surrendered after the Americans dropped two atomic bombs on Hiroshima and Nagasaki. In Canada, the RCAF had trained 131,553 aircrew for the Commonwealth air forces: 72,835 RCAF; 42,110 RAF; 9,606 Royal Australian Air Force; and 7,002 Royal New Zealand Air Force.

B-88, HEESCH, NETHERLANDS

January 1 The New Year started with a bang. The Squadron was at the end of the runway waiting to take off at 0914 hours when forty-plus ME-109s and FW-190s swept across the strip heading due south. Inside of ten minutes, F/O G.D. Cameron returned after shooting down three ME-109s. Shortly after, F/L J. MacKay returned, also with three destroyed, two ME-109s and one FW-190. After running out of ammunition on his first destroyed, MacKay really displayed some fine aggressiveness by chasing the other two a/c so closely that they crashed into the deck. Later in the day, F/L Jake Lee led his section into the circuit of the [German] Rheine aerodrome and came out with one destroyed and one probably destroyed. F/O D.F. Church had one destroyed and one damaged, P/O D.M. Horsburgh one destroyed. The Wing's score for the day was twenty-four destroyed; 401 destroyed nine of these. Total score for the Squadron since D-Day is 76⅓ destroyed, 3 probables, 37 damaged.

January 2 S/L W.T. Klersy [was appointed] the new CO.

January 8 During the afternoon some fifty-odd pilots of the Wing were kept busy shovelling snow off the runways, perimeters and dispersal areas. By the end of the day there were a few sore backs.

January 14   Great joy was experienced by the Squadron who caught a number of FW-190s taking off and landing on Twente aerodrome. The Squadron attacked immediately and five FW-190s were shot down and destroyed. F/L J. MacKay destroyed three of these which brought his score up to seven e/a destroyed and one damaged. F/O D.B. Dack destroyed one and F/L F.T. Murray also destroyed one. F/L R.J. Land was last seen following F/L MacKay over the drome. He did not return and is listed as missing. F/L W.R. Tew came back to us today to start his second tour after a well-earned rest in Canada.

January 15   Some pilots visited the Governor General's Foot Guards Regiment and the 23rd Royal Canadian Artillery units in the vicinity. The pilots got a great kick out of firing the 75mm guns themselves.

January 17   The day was uneventful except that on the second patrol F/L Woods shot down an ME-109 in the Arnhem area.

January 23   The Squadron found a pleasant surprise waiting for them at an aerodrome just north of Osnabruck, where a number of ME-262s were just taking off or landing. Such a target is not very often seen, so after broadcasting the news to any other squadrons that happened to be in the vicinity, they immediately attacked. When the smoke had cleared and the Squadron had returned to base to tally up the score, they found that three ME-262s had been destroyed and six damaged. One jet job crashed while trying to take off so this was also claimed as a damaged.

January 24   After much discussion and having studied all the available recognition material, it has been decided that the jet jobs destroyed yesterday were not ME-262s but a new type called the AR-234. The pilots were not much disappointed.

January 26 The weather was still too duff for any operational flying. This Holland winter weather doesn't make for much flying.

February 11 The weatherman played another request program for Hitler today and kept the "Rams" from making any sorties. [The diary began referring to the Squadron as the Rams after its new crest.]

February 22 Plenty of flak was being thrown up by the enemy on the second [strafing] mission and F/L Freddie Murray's a/c was hit badly. Freddie was forced to crash-land in enemy territory four miles north of Henglo. His actual landing was not seen by any member of the Squadron but we sincerely hope he's OK.

February 24 Hunting was good and a train loaded with lorries, small tanks and armored cars was thoroughly shot up despite the five flak cars it carried.

March 1 Only one mission was carried out by 401 today. But what a show. The Rams while flying with 412 Squadron were bounced in the Dorsten area by forty-plus ME-109s and FW-190s. S/L Klersy, CO of the Squadron, had a field day and got himself three destroyed, two ME-109s and one FW-190, bringing his score up to ten destroyed and two damaged.
[Klersy's combat report read: I was leading 401 Squadron at 12,000 feet when we were bounced. I called a break and positioned myself behind a 109. I opened fire at 500 yards, thirty degrees off, and observed strikes on the fuselage and jet tank, which broke into flame. I closed to 200 yards line astern and fired a two-second burst which resulted in the enemy a/c bursting into flames and spinning down into the deck where it exploded. I got onto another 109 and fired a three-second burst from 300 yards at ten degrees off. There were strikes on the fuselage and wings which finally resulted in the a/c bursting into flames and spinning down to

the deck where it crashed. I then reformed my section and looking about I observed some FW-190s flying above us. I climbed toward them and positioned myself behind one. I opened up at 400 yards fifteen degrees off and didn't see any strikes. I went into line astern and fired a two-second burst observing a strike on the coupe top. The a/c went through a thin layer of cloud in a shallow glide which eventually steepened and went straight into the deck where it exploded.]

The Squadron's success was somewhat dampened with two casualties. F/L Dusty Thorpe was forced to retire from the combat with a badly damaged a/c and barely made it to Volkel where he crash-landed at 195 mph. The Squadron personnel were as happy as Dusty himself when it was known that he scraped through with only a bad shaking up. This is Dusty's last trip and he's been repatted [repatriated] to Canada as tour-expired. Good luck, Dusty. F/L H.P. Furniss was the other casualty. His a/c was apparently damaged in the combat and although he reported over the R/T that he thought he could make it home, nothing has been seen or heard of him.

March 12 F/L L.N. Watt spotted an ME-262 flying merrily along at about 2,500 feet just west of Wesel. He jumped in and after two short bursts saw him going down in smoke. He had to break off the attack then due to very accurate flak from our own guns. The ME-262 was confirmed later, however, by the Army as destroyed. Good eye, Len.

March 13 Just north of Borken, F/O A.R.W. (Bud) McKay reported over the R/T that his engine had packed up and that he was baling out. He went into cloud just at that time and was not seen again. Bud was a quiet chap whose presence will certainly be missed. Good luck, fella, wherever you are.

March 20 Both missions were fighter sweeps in the Rheine-Osnabruck-Muenster area and both proved uneventful. Where are those Jerries?

March 23   The boys were given quite a morale boost tonight. A special briefing was held at 2000 hours for all officers of the Wing. At the briefing we were given information concerning R-Day — the zero hour for the crossing of the Rhine. This push was anticipated to be a very deciding factor in deciding the fate of Germany, not whether she would be beaten, but how soon. It was felt that if the Luftwaffe was to make any appearance in the defence of Germany it would be at this time. Everybody left the briefing room with a clear idea of the importance of the part that this Wing was to play in keeping the Luftwaffe off the backs of our advancing ground forces.

March 24   Five patrols were carried out. But the Hun pilots? Nary a sign. Good news was available in connection with our very popular F/O G.D. Cameron, DFC, who was arraigned before a court martial on a charge of "negligently handling a revolver in such a manner as to cause it to be discharged, thereby injuring F/O Ballantyne, a member of 411 Squadron." The incident took place just after midnight on the 27th-28th January, and the date of the court martial was finally set for today. Everybody knowing of the occurrence considered it an accident and the court, after hearing the evidence, apparently were of the same opinion and F/O Cameron was acquitted with a clear record.

March 28   The Squadron was vectored after enemy a/c in the Coesfeld area shortly after 1600 hours. F/L J. MacKay was the only member of the Squadron who caught up with them. He lost the Squadron in cloud and when he broke cloud spotted six ME-109s. He gave chase to the rear one and destroyed it. While endeavoring to join up with the Squadron, he spotted another ME-109 slipping along the deck. He dropped after it and saw the pilot bale out after his burst of gunfire. F/L Johnny MacKay now has ten e/a destroyed and three damaged to his credit. Nice going, Johnny.

March 30 Misfortune rode with the Squadron today when two a/c pranged when landing. One was an error in judgment and the pilot, F/L W.C. Connell, overshot the landing strip. Bud came out of the accident without injury but it was indeed unfortunate as the trip was to terminate his second tour. The other accident happened when WO1 D.W. Campbell, a newcomer, mistook a ploughed strip to the left of the runway for the landing strip. His a/c nosed over and broke in two but he escaped with a shaking up. As his windshield was oiled up at the time and it was close to dusk, he is being given another chance.

April 2 The Army liaison officer posted everybody up to date on the movements of our fast-advancing armies.

April 4 Two patrols proved quite uneventful and the pilots are showing signs of being anxious to move on up to Germany where there might be a few pickings.

April 6 Bad weather and uneventful patrols are making flying pretty monotonous these days.

B-108, RHEINE, GERMANY

April 12 The Squadron received instructions to pack up and proceed to B-108, Rheine, Germany, and the vehicles got under way at 1215. The Rams ferried twelve a/c to Rheine in the afternoon and got in one eleven-man armed recce after arriving at the new field, [claiming] five transport destroyed and nine damaged.

B-116, WUNSTORF, GERMANY

April 15 Squadron vehicles on the move again. Left B-108 at 1000 hours and arrived at B-116 in the afternoon. The pilots completed a twelve-man armed recce from B-108, scoring one locomotive destroyed and five damaged, two transport destroyed, and thirty-eight transport and thirty rail trucks damaged. The a/c were then ferried to B-116 and duff weather prevented any further operational flying. WO D.W. Campbell crash-landed just north of B-116 [returning from a weather reconnaissance] but was unhurt and brought in safely.

April 16 F/L Johnny MacKay got three AR-234s as they were taking off from an aerodrome and damaged all three. Intense flak forced him to break off the attack.

April 17 Eleven a/c took to the air at 0630 hours on our first armed recce and returned at 0820 hours with one casualty, F/O Len Dunn, who had just rejoined the Squadron at B-108, Rheine, on his second tour of ops. It is believed his a/c was caught in the blast from a petrol train which was being strafed. It exploded and Len was not seen again. He is listed as missing, believed killed. Two more armed recces were carried out and F/O J.P. Francis got an ME-109 destroyed.

April 19 We were "joed" to do four-man patrols over the Elbe, but things brightened a little when one of the patrols led by S/L Klersy spotted a lone FW-190. S/L Klersy bagged it, destroyed. Our boys are gnashing their teeth because they were on patrol while 412 and 402 Squadrons ran into some meaty areas and clobbered a number of FW-190s.

April 20 What a day this turned out to be, eighteen e/a destroyed and six damaged. Our spirits were dampened somewhat, however, by the loss of F/O R.W. Anderson, who was shot down and believed killed on the first do, and F/L B.B. Mossing, who crashed on take-off and was injured.

The a/c were off at 1515 and spotted a large number of e/a taking off from a grass strip southeast of Schwerin with more at 10,000 feet and a top cover at 20,000 feet. The Squadron immediately attacked and when it was all over we had destroyed eleven ME-109s and damaged three more: F/L W.R. Tew and F/O J.A. Ballantine, two each destroyed; S/L W.T. Klersy and F/L L.W. Woods, 1½ each; F/Ls R.H. Cull and J. MacKay and F/Os J.P. Francis and J.H. Ashton, one each.

At 1910 hours the Squadron was off again and this time spotted a large gaggle of enemy a/c taking off from Hagenau aerodrome. They were flying eastward and the Squadron attacked and this time destroyed seven FW-190s and damaged three more. S/L Klersy destroyed two and F/Ls Cull and L.N. Watt and F/Os Francis, G.D. Cameron and D.B. Dack, one each.

April 25   F/L L.W. Woods was knocked down by flak on the first show but he baled out in friendly territory and word has been received that he's safe.

April 29   Patrols over the new bridgehead area across the Elbe were the commitment for the day and three were carried out. No e/a sighted outside of the one that landed here at 0445 hours, the pilot and crew of which surrendered. It was a German JU-52, a transport a/c.

May 1   On the last show of the day one of our a/c flown by F/L G.D. Cameron was hit by flak and Cam was forced to hit the silk. He was seen to land safely in enemy territory and it is hoped that our forward troops in that area will be able to pick him up.

May 2   F/L Cameron was brought back through the lines by a Hun doctor and taken to 124 Wing and then to 81 General Hospital. He was treated for burns on the face and neck.

May 3   A special Squadron patrol [was flown] over Hamburg while the ground forces entered that city. They spotted a grass strip northwest of Kiel with a number of e/a sitting there in various stages of camouflage. The Rams attacked the sitting a/c and meeting with no flak continued attacks until out of ammunition. The total score was twelve JU-52s, two HE-111s and one JU-87 destroyed on the ground. Not bad for a short day's work.

May 4 The first official indication that the war is nearly over was received today. Instructions have been issued that all hostilities on the Second Army front are to cease at 0800 hours on the 5th. However, we are being kept in a state of readiness and further information will no doubt be forthcoming very soon.

May 5 We carried out two four-man patrols before 0800 hours. Both were uneventful.

May 6 No flying carried out today but something new has been added. Our old faithful Spit IXs have been replaced by Spit XIVs from 125 Wing.

May 7 No flying today. Everybody is waiting to hear the official announcement by Churchill that Germany has surrendered. It's understood this announcement will come over the radio tomorrow.

May 8 Still no flying today and Squadron activity consisted mainly of celebrating the surrender of Germany, which was made official today by an announcement by Prime Minister Churchill and a stirring speech by the King.

May 9 The boys are confining themselves to sports activities which haven't as yet got into full swing. Now that the war is over it's anticipated that a lot of time will be spent on sports and suntanning until we can get back home to Canada.

FASSBERG, GERMANY

May 13 The Squadron moved to Fassberg.

May 22 A very heavy blow was dealt to the Squadron today when the CO, S/L W.T. Klersy, DFC and Bar, who has so ably led the Squadron for the past five months, was reported missing on a training flight. He was leading a flight of three a/c when they ran into cloud and he was seen to make a fast turn in the cloud just after issuing instructions over the R/T to the other pilots to climb up through it. When the other a/c flew out of the cloud they could not see S/L Klersy's aircraft and could not contact him on the R/T. It is sincerely hoped that news will soon be received of his safety.

May 25   Official word has been received that S/L Klersy's a/c which was reported missing on the 22nd has been located near Wesel at MR [map reference] E968435. S/L Klersy's body was found in the a/c, burned. F/L E.A. Ker has been appointed to command the Squadron.

The diary does not mention it, but Klersy was believed en route to London for a reunion in the Savoy Hotel of pilots who had served on the Squadron at various times during the war. The pilots did not learn of Klersy's death until after the reunion.

June 23   A signal was received stating that 401 Squadron was disbanded as of this date.

On July 2, 1945, No. 401 Squadron was transferred to 127 Wing. The Squadron flew to England on July 10, and disbanded there two weeks later. Personnel returned to Canada by ship in early August.

EPILOGUE

WHAT DO SOME OF the survivors remember today of their high blue battles?

Senator Hartland de M. Molson of Montreal says that within a few weeks of being pitched into the Battle of Britain in the summer of 1940, No. 1 Squadron became a "well-knit unit with some pride in ourselves, some sadness and concern at our casualties, and a growing conviction that the battle was going to go our way."

He says he recalls little of "hair-raising" aerial combat because at the time there was no time to think. But he does recall the "waiting and sweating" at the dispersal hut before orders came to scramble and intercept far superior (in numbers) German formations.

"I think we were constantly surprised that we were able to hold together. In retrospect, I feel that we represented the country not too badly."

Arthur Bishop of Toronto says: "We were too young to worry much. Do you know what scared me more than the Jerries? It was making some stupid mistake which would get me kicked off the Squadron. We wanted to be and stay part of that Squadron. I still feel that way."

I.F. (Hap) Kennedy of Cumberland, Ontario, now a doctor, shot down fourteen enemy planes and was commanding 401 Squadron in France when flak knocked him down. He recalls: "We were so bloody full of confidence. Our attitude was, 'Let's tear into them.' It didn't matter what the odds were. I think this was because that by this time we were so experienced. In 1944, we had a few rookies, but most of our pilots were already on their second tours of operations. We were a very strong squadron. We could handle the FW-190 and the ME-109 but the flak was hard to avoid. We had a lot of casualties from flak. It made for fast promotion."

R.I.A. (Rod) Smith of Vancouver shot down thirteen enemy planes and, besides, shared in the destruction of the first German ME-262 jet plane brought down by the Allies. He remembers better September 29, 1944, the day after he took over command of 401: "As we started to return from a patrol over the Nijmegen bridge, we came across thirty or so ME-109s harassing a Typhoon squadron. We shot down nine of them without losing any ourselves. It was like swatting them with a tennis racquet. I had never seen so many aircraft hit the ground in such a short time. It brought home to me how good a squadron 401 was."

And he recalls this incident: "One day in 1941, when I was on 412 Squadron, I had a very fierce dogfight with a Hurricane from 401 for twenty minutes. After I landed, I found out that the 401 pilot was the commander, Dean Nesbitt. He was in his late twenties and getting bald. I remember marvelling that such an old man could put up such a great fight."